Catastrophe

Catastrophe

Oy Vey my child is gay
(and an addict)

Anne Lapedus Brest

MF BOOKS
JOBURG

First published by MFBooks Joburg, an imprint
of Jacana Media (Pty) Ltd, in 2014

10 Orange Street
Sunnyside
Auckland Park 2092
South Africa
+2711 628 3200
www.jacana.co.za

ISBN 978-1-920601-36-2

Cover design by publicide
Set in Sabon 11/15pt
Job no. 002180
Printed and bound by CTP Printers, Cape Town

ISO 12647 compliant

See a complete list of Jacana titles at www.jacana.co.za

To Ma, Julie Marcus Lapedus, Queen amongst women,
the most remarkable lady I know.
You will always have my respect and admiration.
I wish I could be more like you.
Ma, this book is for you.

Let me not to the marriage of true minds
admit impediments. Love is not love
which alters when it alteration finds
– 'Sonnet 116', William Shakespeare

When did it begin? And why? When did I begin to notice? And why hadn't I noticed before? And why me? What had I done wrong? They say I wasn't the cause, that it wasn't my fault, and that I couldn't fix it. Then why did I feel so damn guilty?

Contents

CHAPTER 1

Bust

They took her. They put her into an unmarked police car, and drove her away. She was calling wildly out of the window as they sped off.

'Hurry, Mommy! Hurry!'

I stared at the white sedan with its flashing blue light as it made its way down the driveway and finally turned out of view. Disappeared. I stood frozen. Why this? What now? But then, what had I expected? Surely I knew all along that this is where it would all end up? What other ending could there possibly be?

I knew they were taking her to the Morningside Police Station. It's called 'consequences'. My little girl was on her way to prison – except she wasn't so little anymore. She was 36.

Minutes later Helen and I flew into the main entrance of the police station, signposted *SA Polisie* with the post-1994 South African flag flying high. Where to now? We ran into a large room with long, frozen queues snaking at the counters, reporting accidents, thefts, whatever people report at police stations. Some people were scurrying about, others sauntering around, but it seemed as if everyone was shouting, like a flock of maddening magpies.

The noise was deafening. Chaos. The cliché of a 'circus' came to mind, but a circus I didn't want to be at, or part of.

Someone was swiping the floor with a scraggy mop. A young girl was crying loudly, her boyfriend highly agitated by whatever it was that had brought them there.

Helen was totally bewildered. She looked horrified, and sad.

I couldn't stand there waiting in line not knowing where Angela was. I ran into a small side office and stood staring at the guy at the desk, willing him to get off the phone. I could hardly contain myself. Eventually he ended the call and looked up.

'My daughter's been arrested they told us to come here I need to find her where is she where do I go?' I could feel my hysteria rising in my throat. I could hardly breathe. Without answering, he picked up the receiver again, mumbled something into it and then turned to me.

'Auntie, you just go to the second floor and ask for one of the detectives.'

So Helen and I scuttled down the corridors, peering into each of the rooms. I had no idea what I was looking for, or even the name of the arresting officer. I had forgotten to take their names! What if it was a scam and the guys who had picked her up hadn't been police officers at all? Had I asked to see an identity card? It had all happened so fast. Although it was at least 30 degrees outside, I was now freezing, my body clearly retaliating against the trauma.

Where was my daughter? *Where was she?*

I should have seen this coming a long, long time ago. What was wrong with me? I had been warned at all the support-group meetings, the rehab and the counsellors that she could – and would – end up in jail, in an institution or dead. Now she had. Prison. One of the consequences of addiction.

So this was the 'rock bottom' that people had warned me about, the place of no return that I never believed would happen.

'It'll never come to that,' I had convinced myself.

But it had, and here I was, on *Erev Shabbos* – Friday afternoon – half out of my mind, a tumult of angst and rage all but paralysing me. What had she done that she would be arrested? I didn't even know. Would she have to do time? Years? Months? How much time? *And where was she now?* I needed to speak to my brother, and to her father. I wasn't thinking clearly. By now I was shaking, on the verge of hyperventilating, disorientated.

My daughter, the jailbird. Now she'd have a criminal record – one that would mark her for life. How would she ever get a decent job again? Would they feed her properly in prison? What would I tell Ma? Helen was crying softly as she held my arm. She'd worked for us for donkey's years and she'd witnessed Angela's chaos firsthand over the last few years. Why hadn't I listened to those who had begged me to 'do something'? Why had I not believed it when I was told that I was an 'enabler' and a 'co-dependant'? Instead I'd got defensive, angry, and raged about why *I* should carry the blame. *I* wasn't the one doing drugs, *I* wasn't the one stealing, lying – I was doing my bloody best, I was trying to help, trying to be a good, loving mother, trying to do the best by both my children.

So was all of this now my fault? Could I have prevented it? I wasn't even clear about what the charges were. I hadn't been able to follow a thing when she'd been arrested in the driveway earlier.

Helen and I found her eventually – she was sitting arrogantly on the other side of Detective-Constable M's desk, legs stretched out, slouched in the chair, hostile, irritable, abrasive, brandishing a bad attitude and demanding to go home.

They told me she was going to the holding cells and would stay there for the weekend because it was now too late to apply for bail. They told me she had resisted arrest in Douglasdale, and had threatened to set the dogs on the police officers who were arresting her. Charming. They told me she was in a lot of trouble, that she had been accused of stealing a ring worth R40 000 from a friend she had been staying with. They said she had no respect for the law, and no respect for herself. I could have slapped her right there, I swear. She didn't even flinch; they might as well have been talking about someone else. She was not contrite, she showed no remorse, she looked bored – and let everyone know it.

Forms were being filled in, paperwork was being filed, phones were ringing and being answered, life was going on. Helen tried to talk to a woman detective in Sesotho. I remember looking out of the window behind the detective's chair, onto Summit Road. My street, I thought. I live there. It's where I raised my two children. Now it had come to this. Had anybody we knew seen Angela get out of the car in handcuffs?

All the while, as my mind skipped around, I hoped for a miracle that they would let her go. But it soon became clear that that was not going to happen. Then suddenly Detective-Constable M announced that he was taking her to the holding cells and I was to wait in the office.

Angela protested, resisting and shouting as she was hauled off. I was *tsumischt* – finished – beyond exhausted and weary. Thoughts of all the questions from the family, neighbours, wanting answers and the prospect of 'What next?' were now eating me up.

'Mrs Brest?'

'Yes?'

'Come with me, please.'

I followed the policeman down the stairs and out onto a courtyard. I remember that, in my stupor, I slipped as I made my way up a small ramp and hurt myself as I went sprawling, my bag flying open with everything spewing out across the walkway. It must have been hilarious to all those police officers and onlookers hanging around, and I wanted to die.

Humiliated and angry, I managed to pull myself up, gather my things and continue with as much dignity as I could muster, all along my brain trying to work out how it had all come to this. To this place called Rock Bottom.

Rock Bottom, the hellish depths you read about in the Sunday papers, see in the movies, that which happens to other people, not you. Not a nice Jewish family. Rock Bottom, which in my daughter Angela's case now meant prison, full of murderers, rapists, low-lifes, thieves, addicts, wife-beaters, child-molesters, the scum of society, the dregs of the earth.

I had ignored all the warning signs. Of course I hadn't meant to, I had just not seen them or refused to believe them. For the last few years, my brain had been in denial. I knew, but I didn't know. I was an expert at looking the other way.

People often don't want to believe it when news is bad. They convince themselves it's not true, even though the truth is staring them in the face. People especially don't want to know that something is wrong with their children. Denial. The place I seemed most comfortable in.

I was still following the policeman, but had no idea where we were going. Finally, we stopped at a huge iron door. He banged on it, shouted something, and eventually someone on the other side came and opened up. He led me into a cold, windowless room, the smell of stale cigarette smoke almost choking me. And then I saw it. A thick metal grid separating the inmates from the visitors. She was on one side, me on the other.

I could barely make her out in the gloom, but she was there. I heard her. Next to me was a very attractive woman, shouting and arguing with a boyfriend or husband on the other side of the grid. She was screaming at him, accusing him, while he simply pleaded with her, begged her to get him out. I couldn't hear a word Angela was trying to say. Was this really happening? Was this one of my frequent nightmares? Would I wake up soon?

But in the cold light of day, I now knew we were all on this long, hideous road that she had been travelling – a road she had forced us to take with her, a road that lead nowhere, a road bent on hurt and lies and destruction. We were all on it now, without wanting or meaning to be on it. This road that now seemed endless… How were we ever going to escape it?

When did it begin? And why? When did I begin to notice? And why hadn't I noticed before? And why me? What had I done wrong? They say I wasn't the cause, that it wasn't my fault, and that I couldn't fix it. Then why did I feel so damn guilty?

CHAPTER 2

Angela

With thanks and gratitude to Hashem, a darling daughter born 11th April 1975 to Anne (nee Lapedus) and Hymie Brest. Sister for Beverley, Vanessa and Sharleen, granddaughter for Julie Lapedus and Minkie Brest. Thanks to Dr Max Bloom and the staff at the Marymount Nursing Home, Kensington.

That was the announcement in the newspaper. Everyone we knew read it and congratulated us. We were so proud.

She was a beautiful baby, olive skin, a slight slant to her big brown eyes, the legacy gene handed down to her by her paternal great-grandma, Helen Chaya Orkin Brest, of Zagare/Zhager, Lithuania.

She was our little princess, our angel. Angela. We brought her home to 36 Fricker Road, Illovo, and she became the darling of the family. Hymie's older girls, Beverley, Vanessa and Sharleen, from his first wife who died at the age of 28, were thrilled with their new baby sister. They treated her like a doll, they adored her, they saw to her every whim, they fought with each other over who could hold her first, and help bath and change her.

Hymie owned Brest's Exhausts in Fordsburg, Johannesburg, and almost every one of his clients arrived at the house with little pink frocks, babygros, blankets, toys, stuffed animals, baby books, a baby diary and money. She was the centre of everyone's world. She reigned supreme from her little Wonderland nursery, with its imported curtains, fitted sheets, matching wallpaper and gaily coloured compactum. Above her crib was a mobile that played music and turned round and round to lull her to sleep.

She had two doting grannies. Ma, who she called Granny, and Hymie's mother, *Bobba* (Granny) Minkie.

As she grew older, she grew more beautiful, exotic even, and people would stop me in the street and peer into her pram. She spoke at eight months. Walked at 11 months. Our genius baby.

Her brother, Gregory Neil Brest – the little Brest Prince – was born in October 1977. We brought him home, and had him *brissed* (circumcised) in accordance with Jewish tradition eight days later. Gregory was the only boy; he was the only child of Hymie's five children to have green eyes, another adored child in our home.

And so we all lived in perfect harmony for the next few years. Our lives revolved around our kids, our tennis parties, swimming parties, braais, book clubs, pottery classes and 'home movies' on a Sunday night. We were happy. We were. We had our children, and we had each other. What more could we want? But happily ever after is never simple, is it?

Of course it happens to others, and I didn't ever think it would happen to us, but it did... Our marriage didn't work out. I was broken: broken home, broken marriage, broken dreams. Did it matter who was right, or who was wrong? Everyone else had seen it coming, everyone except obliviously happy me. And so, in late 1979, we split up. The older children went with Hymie, and Angela and Gregory with me. I felt enormous guilt at taking my children out of what could have, and should have, been a huge happy and loving home, away from their adoring sisters and their daddy.

Slowly our friends disappeared, all those who flocked over to our endless rounds of braais and swimming parties, our tennis and our movie evenings. Where did they all go, now that we were no longer a couple and not the-people-to-be-with? The only ones who hung around were a handful of Hymie's friends and my very close friends from my single days. They were the ones to whom we clung to help us through.

The younger children and I moved to Ma's lovely little cottagey home in Parkhurst, the house where I had spent many happy years, the house I left to marry Hymie. I needed my mother – she had always been such a stabilising force in all our lives, and she took over totally, because I was a total wreck.

It was a very hard transition for everyone. Nobody in my family had ever been divorced, and now here I was, unable to cope – a failure – a bird with broken wings. I had become an emotional disaster, a mess, a wreck; I could barely look after myself, let alone the children. I had no idea it was going to be like this, that I would fall to pieces. I had no idea I would be so heart-broken. I had been so in love when we married, had so many hopes and dreams for our future. Now it was all about lawyers speaking to lawyers...

For months, all I did was sit in my room, distraught, spending hours on the phone to my girlfriends, whining from morning to night about how difficult life was. And why *me*?

And so it was Ma who took charge of all of us, it was Ma who read to the children at night, and it was Ma who helped me with the lift clubs to ballet and swimming lessons and dental visits. Thank goodness for Ma.

Later I would ask myself over and over again whether this – the divorce, the split and the instability – was the beginning of Angela's problems? Did the damage begin here? I didn't see it.

Angela was such a confident and caring child, one who took everything in her stride. She loved being with Ma and it seemed like life was starting to settle down. But, again, maybe that's what I chose to see. Perhaps she heard my phone calls to her dad, which revolved around our divorce, conversations she may have heard where we spoke endlessly about access and maintenance and who would take what from the Illovo house. Did she hear the death tones? The finality to it all?

After the initial drama, everything became so clinical, so cold, hardly any talking between us except through our lawyers, about court dates, about who got what. The division of spoils. Like the end of a war. A far cry from the fairy-tale wedding, the marriage on which I had pinned so many of my dreams. I was in emotional tatters.

Now whenever I wanted or needed something, Hymie would simply say: 'Have your lawyer call my lawyer.' Was Angela aware of all that? Did it upset her to see that it was her gran who was now the head of the house, not her daddy? Ma tried her best, encouraged me to pull myself together 'for the sake of the children', and to get a job, and start over. She took us on holidays to Umhlanga, Warmbaths (now Bela-Bela), the Eastern Transvaal, Swaziland. She was always there for us; the children adored her – their Super-Gran.

Finally, after months of nothing, I got a half-day job in a photography studio in Sandton City and life seemed to slowly get better. Children adapt easily, but I remember the nights when Angela had frightening dreams and would come to my bed, and I knew that despite her brave little attitude she missed her sisters, her daddy, and the security of what once was our home. What was going on in her mind?

There were so many uncertainties. How would it work? Would Daddy do half the lift schemes and me the other half? Would we split holidays? Birthdays? Would we share the time spent with our children? Whatever our divorce agreement said regarding the visitations and sleepovers, I told Hymie that he could see the children, or take them out, at any time and as often as he liked. I had no intentions of joining the ranks of the 'bitter brigade' of ex-wives who punished their exes through their children. That would just not do.

But, as hard as I tried to look brave, I was heartbroken for my children; it just wasn't supposed to be like this. Hymie never quite took me up on my offer to see the children whenever he wanted, and while they had suppers and sleepovers every Wednesday night, the thrice-monthly weekends didn't always work out. Angela never complained, but I knew it had to have hurt her deeply.

I missed my marriage – I missed being part of a 'couple', missed being a wife and missed the emotional security that my marriage gave me. I was saddened by the fact that my children no longer had their daddy around as often as I imagine they would have liked, and I knew that on the odd occasion that he couldn't have them on 'his weekend' they were hurt and upset – even more so Angela, who was older and could understand. Gregory was too young to notice, I think.

While Angela grew more and more beautiful as she got older, more importantly she developed into a sweet, kind and caring little girl. She was fiercely loyal and protective towards her brother, and looked after him, saw to his every need. She had endless patience with him, and nothing was too much trouble for her when it came to Gregory.

'You want me to get you something, boy?' she would ask in her soft, sweet voice.

It wasn't the easiest of times; it was 1981, a time when there was a huge escalation in the cost of living, and it got harder and harder to earn a good living. In a very short time the child support I had been awarded was worth much less – and that caused some fierce arguments between Hymie and me. Where was my 'escalation clause'? Everyone had that clause in their divorce agreement and I blamed my hot-shot lawyer for the omission. I was furious. He was supposed to be one of the best divorce lawyers of the time, but to be honest I think he traded on his father's good name. His father was a bull terrier, an outstanding lawyer who saw to it that his clients got everything they deserved. His son, however, was another story. But I was stuck with him.

To make matters worse, Angela's daddy soon had a new wife, a new life, and two beautiful daughters, Samantha and Tiffany. A story is made up of many pieces, like a jigsaw puzzle, and in order to explain Angela's life in 1981, I would need to put all the pieces in place, so that the story makes sense. It is hard to sometimes tell the whole truth about other people's lives, especially if it is going to harm them and perhaps others. Today I am acutely aware that these incidents, these parts of the puzzle – often missing ones –

affected Angela deeply. During the writing of this book, she would come out with stuff I had no idea she had known about, rows she had overheard on the phone, and most importantly, the reason for our divorce. These all left a damaging impression on her. She remembered many a weekend when she and her brother, with great excitement, were packed and waiting for Daddy to come, and how sad she felt when the phone call to cancel would come.

Every divorcée knows that it is in very poor taste, and definitely not good for the children, to bitch about Daddy – and certainly not in front of the kids, the innocents in all the mess. But it happened, from both sides. Both Hymie and I would send messages to one another via the children.

'Tell your father the maintenance is late.'

'Tell your mother to pay for the medicine herself! Does she think money grows on trees?'

We were both wrong, but divorce often does that. Of course it upset Angela when I would talk about 'your father this' and 'your father that' when I was angry with him – and I was for many years.

And always, behind everything, it was about money. All the fear around it must have spread around the house. Even though I had a reasonably good job, money was always a hideous, never-ending saga. Money or the lack thereof. The worry, always the worry...

And, despite doing everything I could to make her life as happy as possible, years down the line she would confess that she resented me for leaving her dad. I, of course, had no idea.

Other than a year of madness with a bad choice of a boyfriend – The Bully, we would later call him – in my eyes, life was as normal as could be. Lots of children come from divorced homes, lots of children have fathers living in other countries even. That's what I kept telling myself. Surely things could have been so much worse. But years later when the ugly head of addiction reared itself in Angela's life – in our lives – I was forced to ask myself: Had I really failed so badly as a mother?

In those days, no one even thought of sending a child to a psychologist when one got divorced. It just wasn't done. Everything looked so fine. Who would have known? How many times did my friends tell me how lucky I was that my children are so 'well adjusted' despite everything.

After the divorce I kept a kosher home for the children, following in the traditions of my mother and her mother before her. We had not kept kosher during my marriage. Hymie had done his nut.

'Look at the price of kosher food, man – we must be mad!' Hymie declared one day after we had bought meat for our two maids and gardener, and the family, for the month.

What is it with us Jewish people that a few cents off a chicken is a big deal? I noticed it with so many of the older generation. My mother-in-law would drive to Boksburg to save three cents a pound on a chicken, completely ignoring the *schlep* of getting there, and of course the petrol. She would scour the newspapers for bargains and off she'd go. Boksburg in the East Rand was definitely the place for bargains.

Angela came home one day after *Chader* – religious instruction – and told us she wanted to go to King David in Sandton. I discussed it with Ma who said it was a lovely idea and encouraged it. Hymie, however, nearly had a fit when I told him. He made it quite clear that over his dead body would any child of his go to King David, that the divorce agreement said government-school education (which is true, it did) and the matter was not up for discussion, not now, and not ever and that was his final word. Well, his final word was actually that he would not even 'send his dog to King David'.

Ma liked the idea of Angela going to King David and we spoke about it and she agreed to help with the fees. I also arranged to see Milton Lutrin, who was then on the board of King David, to talk about a possible reduction in fees as there was no way that Ma and I could afford a private school.

'Anne, every Jewish child is entitled to a Jewish education,' Milton said, 'and I'll do my best for Angela.' Milton has a lovely way about him, a gentle person, with a gentle voice. During those early years of my divorce, I was as taut as a stretched elastic band, and it so happened that when people were nice to me, I would become emotional. I was so grateful to him and I beat a hasty retreat before I made a fool of myself by weeping.

So why am I recalling all of this? It's not about looking for blame, but the truth of the matter is that Angela never forgot that I had to get a 'special fees' arrangement to send her to King David.

It *krenked* Angela that she was on 'special fees', she said so over and over, until eventually I brought up the 'not-ever-to-be-discussed' subject of King David with her dad and I got him to agree to take over the account from Ma and me. Oh unhappy days… Over the years there were to be telegrams from the Jewish Board of Education to tell me that the school fees had not been paid. It was so humiliating. I would then go into a mad rant at home, shouting and swearing, forgetting my promise to myself that for the children's sakes, I would never run their dad down in front of them. I really tried not to, but there were times, such as this, when it became impossible not to.

'It's not like Da can't afford it,' Angela said at the table one evening.

It was to remain in her memory, and she speaks of it even today, of the many years of pain it caused her – the bitterness and anguish she felt as a 'charity case'. In years to come, her dad was to send both his younger daughters to King David, and yet he had made such a fuss when it came to her.

'So much for him not sending his dog to King David,' she would bitterly say to me, even when she was in her final year of school and after that.

We joined Rabbi Suchard's *Shul*, the BHH Sandton. Half of King David's children were there. It was great, and it wasn't long before I started meeting what was then a smallish community. Most of the members had children the same or similar ages to Angela and Gregory, and very soon we were being invited for *Shabbos* lunches, to Sunday braais, and our little 'Group' was started. We were known as 'The Group' and I remember those times with much happiness. Although I was single, I felt that I belonged. People had me over – it didn't matter if there were five or seven or nine people.

They didn't think along the lines that I was single and didn't have to have a man in tow. I was me, and I was welcome simply because I was me. These friendships were real and meaningful and solid.

When we walked to the *Shul* every *Shabbos*, the children and I always chatted and I thanked G-d that they appeared to be grounded in spite of the divorce. I finally felt that I had got my life together. I felt more whole, more focused, and pretty much healed from the scars the divorce had left me with. But what about the scars the children had been left with? These were scars I was only to discover many years later.

One particular *Shabbos* morning, up Summit Road, past the Morningside Police Station, into Rivonia Road and all the way along to the *Shul*, we had a conversation I will never forget.

It started with Greg asking, 'What was Ireland like, Mom?' I told them of the freezing winters, with winds coming in from the North Pole that Granny hated. I told them about my loving grandparents, my cat, my life, and I told them that I love them unconditionally.

Neither one of them knew the meaning of the word 'unconditionally', so I gave them the first example that came into my head: 'Let's say, G-d forbid, when you get older, and you were arrested and had to go to prison, Mommy would bring chicken soup to you in your cell.'

And they got it. What an absurd answer, but that's what sprang to mind at the time.

CHAPTER 3

Bat Mitzvah and boyfriends

The King David girls were preparing for *Bat Mitzvah* Day. This is the day they stand in *Shul* and recite beautiful pieces in both English and Hebrew, when they become women in the eyes of Hashem and the community. It was a wonderful time for Angela, and there was much excitement among the girls. The mothers formed a committee to discuss their outfits, and there was a lot of *kugelling* and *kibitzing* – heckling – over the colour schemes and fabrics and what to wear and what not to wear. Eventually, after many meetings and discussions, the decision was that the girls would wear white with turquoise and lace. According to convention, the skirts had to be no shorter than knee length and the girls had to have their shoulders covered. Most of the *kugels* were having their kids' dresses made but money was still rather tight for me, so because I was good on the sewing machine I ran up a beautiful dress for Angela, and she loved it. It was white with big, puffed sleeves, and a turquoise belt with a bow at the back. I added a little turquoise trim around the square neck of her dress. She looked so sensational.

The *Bat Mitzvah* ceremony was held at the Sandton *Shul* on

Sunday, 7 September 1987. The service was lovely and, watching from the ladies' section, I cried heartfelt tears along with all the other King David *Bat Mitzvah* mothers. Naturally, Hymie Brest sat downstairs with the rest of the men. We watched proudly as our beautiful little girl took her rightful place as a woman, in accordance with our *Torah*, Jewish Law, and she read her portion in a clear and confident voice.

After the ceremony, and photo shoot that followed, we had a party for Angela in the garden at home, where she made a beautiful speech. Oh happy days – we were all so proud of her. It felt good, like we all belonged to the greater King David community.

But while the children loved it there, King David Sandton could be a real pain in the neck for some parents. A lot of the mothers were *kugel* stereotypes who spoke with nasal voices, never failed to dress to the nines, and swept into the school grounds in magnificent cars. Not all of them, of course, but many. Every hair in place, long painted nails, name-brand gym outfits, all Jane Fonda look-a-likes and wannabes. They hit the gym in the mornings, made regular visits to the hairdressers, scheduled appointments for manicures and pedicures, made use of their time share in Umhlanga every July, took holidays in Cape Town at the end of the year, and of course at least one annual overseas trip thrown in for good measure. Everyone made arrangements for their kids to get together later in the 'arvy'.

Having the children at King David was wonderful in many ways, but hard in others. There was always that peer pressure. Many of the King David children would go overseas for the December holidays, only to come back and have another holiday down in Cape Town or Umhlanga so that the parents could relax after *schlepping* around England or the USA or wherever they had gone. So it was that in early 1988 Ma suggested that she and I split the costs and take the children to Chicago, Disneyworld and Florida. There was a huge family gathering because my brother and sister-in-law were going too and there was lots of planning. And we did go – and it turned out to be wonderful in every way. At last we had joined the jet-setting Jewish community!

In the mid-1980s, when Anglela was 11 and Gregory was nine, I ended a relationship with a good-looking, charming albeit self-centred guy, only because I didn't feel he would be good 'father material' for my children. I then took up with a fat, ugly bloke, with a daft sense of humour, and firmly resident, certainly financially, in Nowheresville – not a good combination, I know, but I was tired of the '*gorjus*' selfish men, the ungratefuls and the unfaithfuls, and I thought that if I married this man, he'd be good to my children and faithful to me. He was neither. He was the one who was later dubbed The Bully.

He turned out to be a nightmare, his erratic behaviour bordering on sheer lunacy. It soon became clear that he had serious control issues and it wasn't long before he revealed himself to be a religious zealot – and yet, hypocritically, thought nothing of sending me flying with a back-hand one miserable evening, for no reason other than his own out-of-control temper.

That was the first time.

So why did I marry him? In fact, why did I have to remarry at all? So that my children would have a father figure at home. Surely I would have, and should have realised that this guy was a nutter? What right did I have to drag my children into this? I spent many years blaming myself for this monumentally bad decision. Because it was my fault – nobody held a gun to my head. Even a well-known rabbi tried to warn me. But I didn't listen… The signs were all there. On the radar. Why had I not seen them?

His apologies and promises that it would never ever happen again kept me in the marriage for the next three sickening years. Then he lost that mad temper of his and, like a raging bull, pounded his big fat fists into my head the night before *Kol Nidre*. Angela heard me screaming and rushed to my assistance but in the scuffle that ensued he twisted her hand and broke two of her fingers.

He wouldn't let us out of the house. He locked the doors, ripped phones out of the walls and threatened to kill us both. Gregory was sleeping at a friend. Fortunately, with the help of our domestic, I managed an escape and, with Angela in tow, tore down the highway in a nightmare-from-hell drive with him in hot pursuit. Hospital security helped us inside because The Bully, now maniacal, was trying to prevent us from entering. Then doctors, X-rays, questions, more questions, me calling our friends to warn them to hang on to Gregory and not allow him to go with anyone except *me*, because the lunatic Bully had threatened to go there and collect my son. That same night I ran into the police station in Morningside, the same place where Angela was later to spend three nights on a cold stone floor, to report it, and there and then, that same night, I removed The Bully from my life and the lives of my children, never to return.

By the time we eradicated The Bully from our lives, Angela was in Grade 9 at King David Victory Park. She was a natural at sports, including netball and swimming, and by the time she reached Grade 11, a nice boy had plucked up the courage to ask her out and she was absolutely delighted. Angela had a boyfriend! She told me all about him and they had their school photo taken together. He was lovely – warm and caring, with a generous heart. They spent all their time together, and his family loved her; she was the daughter they never had.

In 1992, Angela finished school and went off to study Oral Hygiene at Wits. She would go on to get her Honours there, too, and we were all immensely proud of her. We all went down to Wits, armed with cameras, and took photographs, with Angela bowing to the Dean on one knee, humbly accepting her degree.

Now my Angela was all grown up. She got her first job in a very successful dental practice in Randburg, running around in a little car she bought for herself. Her life revolved around her career, her family, her boyfriend, his family and their wonderful friends. It was a great time; life was wonderful. We all went to Warmbaths (now Bela-Bela) on long weekends, braaied and laughed together. His family took her to Israel and we took him to Umhlanga. We had joint holidays in Cape Town, two families joined together by our beloved children. We had such hopes and dreams.

When Boyfriend went overseas for a year to study further, Angela was lonely without him and missed him terribly. Then in 2000 Boyfriend came back and we all went to Cape Town on holiday. Everyone was there. The weather was great and we spent our days soaking up the sun on Camps Bay beach. By this point things looked serious between Angela and Boyfriend, who was talking about studying in the States for a while and then settling in Israel.

'Looks like you and I won't exactly be bringing the young couple chopped liver on Friday nights,' Boyfriend's mother laughed as she handed me a cheese-and-tomato bagel from the cooler bag on the beach.

The sun was shining, reflecting off the pristine white sand and as I lay back and looked up at the world-famous mountain range, the most magnificent in the entire world, I don't think I had ever felt happier.

CHAPTER 4

Oy vey, my child is gay

Angela and Boyfriend were planning a joint celebration of their 25th birthdays at Jabula, a recreation hall in Sandringham. Their birthdays were a few weeks apart and I was convinced it was going to be a combined engagement party. I didn't ask, but waited instead with baited breath... The young couple saw to most of the plans themselves, and catering preparations were well underway. On the night, disco music belted out and the young people had a blast, partying well into the night.

But there was no engagement, no announcement – just nothing. And I thought to myself, if not now – when? Oh well, maybe they were waiting until the end of the year. Actually, it might be better if they announced it then because my aunties, uncles and cousins were all coming over from the United States, and my Auntie Freda was coming from Canada, to celebrate Ma's 80th. It would be the perfect time to announce the engagement. Ma was really keen on the idea and talked about it often: a wedding presumably in August or September, just in time to go to the United States where Boyfriend wanted to study for a year at some American business school.

But instead of the dream wedding announcement, there was a bombshell. Soon after their joint birthday bash, Angela and Boyfriend broke up. She came to tell me one afternoon when I was sitting at the computer. A bit of mumbling at first, I couldn't make head or tail of what she was saying, but once she slowed down and came out with it, the *untester shurer* – the gist of it – was that she had ended her eight-year relationship with Boyfriend, something about having issues she needed to sort out.

'What do you mean, you broke up?' I demanded, getting up from the computer as I walked over to her.

She explained she had some serious issues and wanted to work through them with a therapist. I wondered why they couldn't have worked through the 'issues' together, but she said she 'needed space' and theirs was just 'a temporary break-up'. I asked her if the 'issues' had something to do with Boyfriend, but she assured me that it had nothing at all to do with him, not in any way, just something that was worrying her, her own 'stuff' – as she called it. I just shook my head in total disbelief.

'Try to understand, Mommy.'

But I didn't understand at all. Why break up just to deal with some 'issues'? What issues? He was a wonderful boy, so good to her – and for her. They seemed so in love. They were inseparable. What issues could she have? Nothing serious, that's for sure.

We were all upset, his family and I – puzzled and confused by it all; none of it made any sense. I felt such a loss, because if it was not going to be him, then who? He was superlative, a first-class young man, clever (brilliant, actually), from a lovely family. Plus, our families were so close.

It was barely a week later that she came home one evening with a scrawny character. At first, I wasn't sure if I was looking at a boy who was effeminate or a girl who was masculine. Then I recognised her as one of the guests at the joint birthday party. Apparently she had huge emotional issues, and Angela was her chosen 'rescuer'. Angela knew I'd be sympathetic when she told me her friend suffered with panic and anxiety, because I too suffered with both, and so when she kept bringing her home to 'help her' deal with the anxiety I was sympathetic, but I had a very bad feeling... And not just bad, terrible.

The friendship, however, continued. Angela's new young friend was at our home a lot of the time and then she began to sleep over almost every night. In the mornings after Angela had left for work, she would sit in my room and drink her coffee. She was a nice enough young woman, chatty, talented, a muso, a singer of some sort (she'd cut a CD). She was popular and had a huge following, mainly among teenagers and twenty- and thirty-somethings (I had never heard of her before), and she was pretty in a boyish sort of a way. After about six months of this odd friendship, I heard myself asking Angela if she and the scrawny girl were involved in any way. I am not sure where I got the courage. Angela bit my head off, and denied it all. She asked how I could even dare suggest this, that she was helping her with her panic and anxiety and that was it. I felt awful for having asked.

Boyfriend called me a few times, devastated, and asked me what he had done wrong. He couldn't understand why they were not working through Angela's 'issues' as a couple. And I agreed – I simply could not understand it at all. It didn't make sense. And Ma! *Oi vey*, that was another story. She was *tsumischt*. Totally.

I was due to fly to the USA but about a week before I left I had a chat to Angela. I tried to make it as casual as I could, like it wasn't a big deal.

'Ang, uh... When I get back from the States I hope that your... uh... friend will have moved out. Enough is enough – aren't her parents worried about her? Shouldn't she be at home with them?'

And when I got back from the States, she was gone all right – and so was Angela. Not officially 'moved out', as such – her things were all still there – but she hardly spent a night at home for weeks. So what did that tell me?

Eventually word started going around that Angela and her 'friend' were an item. They were seen together holding hands, seen together in Plett, seen together in Cape Town, and at concerts. I couldn't take it all in. For eight years she had appeared to be so happy with Boyfriend. It was 'babe' this, and 'babe' that. They laughed together – a lot – and spent so much time with each other, I was convinced they were soul mates. She adored him, respected him. What could possibly have gone wrong? They hadn't even argued. And now she had replaced him with this scrawny, boyish girl.

I always liked to think that no matter what my children told me, I would be accepting of it. But the truth of the matter is that I went mad. How could this have happened? From having a boyfriend for eight years to suddenly going around with gay men and women?

It was during this time that most of Angela's friends, and my friend's daughters, were getting engaged. All the kids from the old crowd were dating seriously, and engagements led to marriage, and then babies. I found that a hard and bitter pill to swallow. My friends would call, shrieking from excitement, to tell me that their daughters or their sons had just got engaged; I too wanted to phone my friends, shrieking with the excitement of it all, host an engagement party for her, plan a wedding, a wedding dress, have a son-in-law, a grandchild, grandchildren.

Would I ever walk my daughter down the aisle? Would I ever hold my daughter's son, a grandson, in my arms and be a part of his *bris* (circumcision), where baby, his father, and his grandfather, too, would dress in their *tallis* – prayer shawl – while the baby was being named. Men would stand with tears in their eyes, and what a beautiful sight to behold as the child is handed to his grandfather. As a baby, every boy has his *bris*, and carries the name of his ancestors, the 'Tribe' of his father, and his father before him, going back to the earliest generations, in Lithuania, Latvia, and the various European countries where Jews have lived for centuries. And one day, this baby boy will name his own son in precisely the same way. This is our tradition.

And now there would be nothing.

I had always thought – naively, I suppose – that if you were gay, you were born that way; you didn't just 'turn' gay at the age of 25, out of the blue. Or did you?

I remember a woman who lived in the same townhouse complex

told me once that she had come home one afternoon to find her husband in bed with another man. And the cousin of a close friend had left her husband for a woman. So this was it then.

Of course, I wasn't so naïve or so ignorant to think that I had never encountered gay people before. I'm sure I had – many times. At school, I remember how we would snigger if we saw a 'queer' prancing around, or butch dyke women dressing and acting like men. As girls, we used to laugh and say to one another, 'Les-be friends'.

So for my generation and preceding ones, and in my middle-class suburban world, gay people remained – for the most part, anyway – firmly behind closet doors. The terms 'liberation' and 'equality' and 'acceptance' were the territory of the struggle against apartheid. It never occurred to me (or, truth be told, those in my social circle) that it would apply to sexual orientation. It wasn't something I encountered in my day-to-day environment and, as such, not an issue I was ever compelled to deal with in any personal or practical way whatsoever. I knew gay people existed, and that was that. And if the issue of homosexuality raised its head on any sort of social context where we were ever forced to face it, it was usually in hushed tones and behind cupped hands, a wink and a smirk and a knowing nod. Slowly, however, I was coming to the realisation that the matter touched much closer to home than I had ever imagined it would. Those whispers now echoed from behind my own front door. How would I ever be able to encounter them? Could I?

I'd met some of Angela's new friends, effeminate young men, and manly looking women. Women who walked with a rolling gait, hands thrust deep in their pockets, hair cut short like a boy's, wearing what were essentially men's clothes. These young women sat the way men sit, smoked cigarettes the way men smoke, and drove cars like men, gripping the steering wheel with one hand, elbow out of the window. Angela wasn't like that at all; she had long hair, she was beautiful, girly.

I tried to be 'cool' about it, of course, but it wasn't working. I came out with a question one day. We were sitting at Village Walk.

'Why don't you have hormone treatment or something?' I asked her, sipping a cup of Milo that was so hot it scalded my throat. Shite. No sooner were the words out of my mouth than I realised I had said the wrong thing.

She looked at me, those beautiful slightly slanted Brest eyes flashing at me, dark pools of darkness behind them, anger, and ridicule. She was furious, I could see that, and I wish I hadn't opened my big mouth and said it, but once I had, I couldn't take it back.

And what was I going to tell Ma? As it is, Ma had never quite got over the break-up of the 'lovely young couple'. She asked me constantly if I couldn't 'do something' to 'put it all back together again'. Like Humpty Dumpty or something. We even argued about it sometimes.

'Ma, for heaven's sakes!' I'd tell her, far more irritable than I should be. 'Let it go already.'

My brother Robert sometimes picked me out for being irritable with Ma, but when she started in on Angela and about her getting back with her boyfriend, I lost it.

Poor Ma, it was a pity for her really. She was from another generation, and as difficult as it was for me to learn to accept it all, it was twice as difficult for Ma. She was old school, born in 1920 in Ireland, a devoted daughter, wife, mother and gran. She never swore, never said a bad word about anyone, ever. Everyone loved her. She had been widowed in 1963, two years after we arrived in South Africa, at the age of 42. My dad was only 47 when he died suddenly after an operation to repair a heart valve. My grandfather wanted us to go back to Ireland, but Ma was stoic. She had a good job, and felt that it would be better for Robert and me to make a go of it here in South Africa, the land of sunshine and golden opportunities, where the sun shone and the sky was blue, and life was easier than it had been in Ireland.

She hated the cold, wet Irish weather, gale winds blowing in from the North Pole, under our front door, howling throughout the house, the snow and the sleet, the slush. I remember her falling once, when I was about five, slipping on the ice on the way home from buying a bottle of milk and hurting her back.

It had been a wrench for her to leave her Mammy and Daddy, my grandparents, behind in Ireland, and all that was familiar to her in our close-knit little Dublin Jewish community, but she did it for us, Robert and me, and for my Da. Da had a huge family based in South Africa, all wanting us to come to here, to start a new life, away from the cold and damp of Ireland, away from the loss of Da's optical shop in a fire in 1952 when I was just six – a fire that was to change all our lives forever. Da got sick soon after that, and it was then that the seed to leave Ireland and move to South Africa was sowed.

Ma never got over leaving her parents behind, and she felt terribly guilty about it. She had been the last remaining child in Dublin, her siblings having all moved off in the early 1950s. For Da it was a different kettle of fish – half his family were in South Africa. And so he made his way south, leaving Ireland, with a plan in mind to bring us all out in the February of 1961.

But here in the 21st century Ma would never, could never, understand how or why her 'beauty' had 'chosen' this very different path. To be gay. To love another woman. And by the time Angela told us she was moving out of home, it was becoming clearer that this was no passing phase, no impulsive whim on the part of a petulant or curious twenty-something intent on 'finding herself' by experimenting with an alternative lifestyle. That much was for sure. And by this point I knew it too.

Angela had found a lovely place somewhere off Katherine Street in Sandown, and she felt it was time to move out. Unbeknown to me, she was going to be sharing the townhouse with a young woman – not the scrawny little panic sufferer, but another woman, also with boy-girl looks, short hair and a very boyish body. A woman, in fact, I'd seen her with once, albeit from a reasonable distance. Michelle. Whereas I had liked the panic sufferer, I didn't like the look of Michelle. She had a sneaky look and a shifty way about her.

Angela started coming around to see me every now and again, no longer so angry. She seemed to have gotten over the 'Village

Walk' incident, and I was trying to be 'cool' and to 'go with the flow'. One evening when I was out photographing some event or other, she brought Michelle to the house. She left a huge box of Ferrero Rocher chocolates (my favourites) for me on the dining-room table. I came home and found it there, with a note pinned to it, but I pushed the box aside. I knew Michelle was just trying to *schmooze* me, win me over – and to make it worse, our beloved dachshunds managed to get up onto the dining-room table and, between the two of them, neatly took each Ferrero Rocher chocolate out of its gold-foil wrapping and ate themselves sick. Literally. Right then and there, on the carpet, all over the lounge, into the passage and up the stairs to my bedroom, a malfunction that not even the best drycleaner in the world could sort out. So I tiled the lounge floor, but it cost me money I didn't have, and I hated this Michelle with a new-found venom.

Angela finally 'came out', not exactly with 'I'm gay' but rather that she was just 'going through a girl phase', like experimenting; it wasn't forever, but 'for now'. Now having said it, named it, she admitted that it was indeed the reason why she ended her eight-year relationship with Boyfriend. It was why she had gone to see the therapist and that was the 'issue' she had been dealing with.

And for Michelle, it was *min dae* – her days were numbered and she didn't last that long. Their relationship had always been a volatile one, and she caused the most awful problems: pitching up uninvited to Angela's work, making scenes, shouting, threatening, screaming, it was all horrendous. Once she even had to be escorted off by the security guard. Thankfully, Angela dumped her.

After that all kinds of friends came and went. And it was becoming clear to me that I had to change my attitude and be more accepting. It was either that, or lose my daughter. It was that simple. Once Angela had actually 'come out' I knew I had to change my entire focus. I had to make her friends feel welcome. I loved my daughter, and wanted her in my life, and I wanted to be in hers, and I knew that if I didn't think and see things differently, she would not want to be around me, she would continue hiding her lifestyle from me.

G-d, I was devastated. Depressed. I never saw it coming. It was like my whole world had collapsed around me. I didn't get it. I kept hoping that she would decide that it was indeed just a phase, like the movie star Anne Heche, who claimed to be straight, then gay, then straight again. That's what I hoped. I knew someone from Yeoville who had been boy-mad, then went gay, then straightened out and got married. Had a set of twins and three more children. Maybe this was just a passing phase for Angela too.

But phase or not, I knew I had no choice but to go with the gay flow; I had to be 'cool' and embrace it, because I couldn't possibly bear losing her. It was nevertheless eating me up.

I started going to see gay movies with her, I photographed Mr and Miss Gay World, I photographed gay weddings and, after a while, it all started to feel commonplace. I wasn't so acutely aware of it any more, the girl-boys, and boy-girls, and men in dresses with make-up and long painted fingernails. I mean that although I did notice it, it started to become more 'normal' to me when I was with the gay crowd. I realised that I had become more sincere in welcoming Angela's friends into our home. To my surprise, many of the women were very girly-looking; many wore make-up and dresses (Angela called them 'lipstick lesbians'). So it was that I slowly became much more accepting. I mean, what else could I do?

I resigned myself to the fact that it would all be good – well, for Angela anyway. And, as she so rightly said, it wasn't about *me*, it was about *her*, and her happiness, and would I have wanted her to be unhappily married to a man, or happily involved with a woman? So that was what I focused on, the thought that would get me through all those sleepless nights: that I was happy that she was healthy, that she was happy.

But was she happy? I know she missed her brother Greg and felt abandoned when he had left for America. They were close.

Around 2005 Angela moved into an apartment with her hairdresser, an Afrikaans-speaking guy from Pretoria, with dyed white hair, a crazy dress sense, and an accent so thick that at first I thought he was putting it on. I had met his father when they first moved into their new place, safari suit, the same accent, and a comb stuck into his sock – in fact, the stereotype Afrikaner of all those Van der Merwe jokes. But Angela and her hairdresser were best friends, companions; they were there for one another. Neither was involved with anyone else, and not physically involved with each other, so their relationship worked well for them. It started off as a really warm friendship, so I saw past the dyed hair, the accent and the affectations, and was happy that Angela had such a good and caring friend. He seemed quite sweet actually, and I liked him.

When he and Angela would come every Friday night for *Shabbos* dinner, Ma would ask again and again whether she and her hairdresser were an item.

'No, Ma, not at all. They're just... uh... good friends. Like platonic, you know.'

Ma wanted to know why Angela was not dating – after all, it was a good while since the break-up with Boyfriend, and surely it was time for her to move on. But instead of gently explaining that Angela was not yet ready to date, I would get irritable with Ma. Of course, I knew full well why she wasn't dating in the sense Ma was talking about, but the family decision at the time, and Angela's, was not to tell her that Angela was gay.

But Ma is a very wise, astute person, and she was well aware of the fact that Angela never took a date to any of our family weddings. Both my brother's sons got married, one older, one younger than Angela. Angela would go alone to the weddings.

Except for the Jewish High Holidays, *Rosh Hashanah* and *Yom Kippur*, she came less and less often to *Shul*, and although she did keep kosher in some of her homes, I think it started to wane after a while. And even though she did have a *mezuzah* – a piece of parchment inscribed with specified Hebrew verses from the *Torah* and placed in a protective casing – on her front door, she became not only disinterested, but almost cynical about her Judaism, complaining that Jews were loud and noisy, that so many Jewish girls were *kugels*, their kids spoilt rotten. Of course, there was an element of truth to that, but still it hurt me. I let it go, though. I mean, what could I do? She was already a young woman, and it saddened me that she would not one day hand the Jewish tradition to a child born to her. Did being gay mean you couldn't have a child of your own? I hoped she would have a baby or two, grandchildren for me. I wanted that so badly. Of course I wasn't stupid enough to say it out loud, but she knew it, not from anything I said, but because every woman wants that. Well, at least most...

Angela loved her gran very much, and spent a fair amount of time with her. They'd go to movies together, and she'd go to her at least one night during the week for supper. They had a very special bond, always laughing together, and Angela was gentle to her, adored her, a kind and loving granddaughter. She was always 'Gran's little beauty'.

In 2008 and with a wonderful farewell from the dental practice, Angela moved on to marketing and landed a wonderful job. She was always so efficient and smart, and had been headhunted. In fact, she did so well that she was given a raise in her first month. She always had her head screwed on right, so down to earth. So solid.

She was now dating a lovely young woman, pretty, grounded, talented, warm and well spoken. Not long after they met, they moved in together. Lionel, my partner since 2007, and I went to the house-warming party. It was a beautiful old place in Kensington, and I fell in love with the wooden floors, the high ornate ceilings, the large stoep, the nostalgic feeling of early Johannesburg, the scent of jasmine, a dog barking in the distance. People were sitting around in groups: theatrical young men sipping cocktails, women with their hands wrapped around a can of beer and willowy young professionals with beautiful figures and long hair. There was laughter, burning candles, gentle music, and drinks for all.

I must admit I felt a little out of place when we arrived – what with me being Angela's mom, and my partner Lionel in tow, but one has choices in life: we can choose to fit in and go with the flow – or not. I chose to fit in, and be part of it all. I gave everyone bear hugs, Lionel shook their hands, and we actually enjoyed the evening. Angela went out of her way to make us welcome. We sat out on the patio; it was a lovely evening, the air fresh and the sky ablaze with an African sunset. We chilled, enjoying the vibe, the aura, the conversations, but most of all, I was happy to see Angela happy. Even though it would take some time to come to terms with her life choices, it goes without saying that a mother is happy when her child is healthy and happy.

Happiness, however, is a fleeting thing; it can be here today and gone tomorrow, and as a friend of mine (who took her own life about 10 years ago) once said, 'When you find happiness, grab it with both hands.' I wanted Angela to be happy – she's my gorgeous daughter, and I love her so much. She was so grounded and sensible; I wished I could have been more like her. I am far too emotional for my own good, far too anxious, always worrying about things that often never happen. Angela, on the other hand, was practical, sensible, solid, salt of the earth, a good citizen. She didn't take after me at all!

So she and her beautiful girlfriend lived together in their Kensington home; they came to me every Friday night for *Shabbos* supper, and Ma came as well, sometimes visitors. Ma, I'm sure, realised that this was not just two gal pals together all the time; she knew they lived together, but what she didn't know was that they shared a bedroom. She must have worked it out, although it was never spoken of. Angela didn't want to tell her, and I went along with it. Occasionally my brother and sister-in-law raised the issue of telling her. What if she found out, heard it somewhere? And, besides, she was no fool, surely she had worked it out? But Ma was not as young as she used to be; she was a lot more frail. Would she be able to handle it all? Robert, Sharon and I had this discussion often, but in the end, it was always decided it was best not to tell her. What if her blood pressure went up, or she went into some kind of emotional slump, like she had after Angela broke up with Boyfriend?

CHAPTER 5

Missing

When was it exactly that I started to notice? The money missing from my purse? It had probably been going on for a while but I hadn't been aware of it. Perhaps it was because I never keep much money on me. In fact, I wasn't even sure I was missing money, because I never counted the money I carried anyway. Sometimes, though, I would have a mental picture of a few fifties and twenties and maybe a hundred-rand note. And now there were just a few twenties. Oh, well, maybe I never had it in the first place; I probably spent it, didn't I? There had been a few times when I'd thought I had more money in my purse than I actually had, but, then again, maybe I didn't. Money came and went, everything was so expensive, you go to Pick n Pay, buy two things, and before you know it, you've blown R200. So that is what must have happened.

I suppose, now that I think back, money had been disappearing for a good while. But then again, maybe not: I was careless, always losing things – that was just me. Then, in February 2008, when I went to New Zealand with Lionel, my brother gave me a US$100 bill the day I left – just for 'in case'. But I didn't spend it and brought it back to South Africa with me. The day after we returned, I decided to cash it in but when I got to the bank, it wasn't in my wallet. Silly me, I thought, I must have left it at home.

I went home to look for it, and searched all over the place: in my passport wallet, my cupboards, my carry-on luggage, my suitcase, under the bed, in pockets, in other handbags, I searched everywhere. I even called the taxi that had brought us back from the airport thinking I might have by mistake handed it to the driver as a tip. Maybe I dropped it on the floor of the cab? I searched my suitcases, and then my wallet a second time around, and even a third. And all the time I blamed myself for being careless.

Ma was right all those years ago when, as a child, she used to say, 'Anne, if your head wasn't screwed on your shoulders, you'd lose it'.

I once went to see a movie at the Rosebank Mall with my cousin, Charlene, and when I opened my purse to reimburse her for the tickets it was empty – not a cent. Nothing. Nada. How could that be? I would never have gone out without a cent in my purse. Didn't my father drum it into my head from when I was a kid that one never goes out with an empty purse? Even just to have a few bucks for the taxi should I ever need one in a hurry. And yet here I was, blathering away to Charlene that I was so sorry but I had no money.

But now it kept happening, money missing, missing, missing. I seemed to be always looking, looking, looking. I had Helen looking too. We were always searching. One day, just as a little exercise, I decided to count the money in my wallet... So I did. R170. And because I was starting to distrust my own memory, I wrote it down on a piece of paper. Angela was coming over that evening and when she left, I hurried off to count the money. There was just R70. There was R100 missing. Immediately, of course, I doubted myself and thought that I must have just counted it incorrectly, that it was never R170 to start off with, that it was just R70. My mistake, *mea culpa*.

It was driving me crazy. I thought I was losing my mind. Nothing changed no matter how careful I was. I was still missing money, and still always searching, always looking, but now in the oddest places, convinced I was losing my marbles: under the bed, behind the couch, under the seats, in the linen cupboard, in the studio, in the kitchen cupboards, in jacket pockets. I got so tired from always looking for my money.

One day Hymie called.

'Do you ever miss money?' he asked. 'Because, man, I tell you, money has gone missing here – even the maid's money that Felicité left for her on the kitchen table is missing, and there is nobody here but us.'

'Hymie, wait, I'll ring you back.'

I couldn't think straight, my head was spinning. *What was going on?* How could it be that Hymie and Felicité were *also* missing money? Immediately my mind said, 'Well, it's a bloody coincidence, that's all it is.'

But was it?

I couldn't even think through all the scenarios that were pounding in my head. I started to think about the fact that my credit card had been used while I was in New Zealand. Of course, the bank had reimbursed me with a credit, but that's not the point. Who had been using my card? And even after I got back from New Zealand, my card was still showing purchases that were not mine? Or were they? Maybe I'd forgotten that I bought a green marble cigarette lighter for R600? But why would I have done that – I don't even smoke. No, it wasn't me.

I started making phone calls to garages, to stores, going to the places where the purchases were being made. I was like a detective, consumed by the mystery of it all. What was happening? I used to skype Gregory in America, but he laughed it off to the fact that I had always been a 'bit of a *loskop*'. Yes, that was it. Nothing to worry about.

But in the back of my mind I knew that something was very, very wrong. I wasn't losing my marbles, so what was going on? Why was money disappearing? And where was it going? Who was taking it? So I thought about it logically. It certainly wasn't Lionel, it certainly wasn't Helen, and it certainly wasn't me.

I never thought I would do this – or *could* do this – and I'd never done it before, not to Ma and Da when I was a child, not to my brother, not to Hymie, but I started opening Angela's mail. I'd never opened a letter belonging to anyone in my life, but now I was doing it. I felt terrible. Sneaky, mean, sly, underhand and pathetic. I started off by steaming open the envelopes. There were bills, huge bills – she seemed to be in so much debt. I couldn't understand it because she had a fabulous job, and yet all her accounts were in arrears. Everything. I would seal the envelope again and hand her the mail on Friday nights when they came for supper.

I didn't tell Lionel. In fact, I didn't tell anyone, I just kept on doing it, and each month I could see she was getting deeper and deeper into the red. Then I started to simply open the envelopes by hand and glueing them closed with Pritt. She never noticed.

So Angela was heavily in debt. But lots of people are, it didn't mean anything sinister; it just meant she was not managing her money properly. That's all. But still I wondered what she was doing with the money. I simply couldn't imagine where it was going. I could no longer keep quiet about it so I eventually told my brother and sister-in-law about my suspicions and my snooping. They asked me the same question I was asking myself: What's happening to all her money? Robert was also adamant that this couldn't continue, and that something was clearly wrong, very wrong.

'You think she's gambling?' he asked one afternoon as we were having something to eat at The Cup in Morningside. I just shook my head. I didn't know what to think any more.

I asked her one day if she was okay, whether she was in any kind of trouble or anything, and offered to give her a loan, but she assured me that she was 'good' and didn't need a loan at all.

Kol Nidre night, October 2008, Angela came over for an early supper so we could begin the yearly *Yom Kippur* Fast, the Day of Atonement. We left the house around 5.30pm in separate cars and agreed to see one another in a few minutes at the *Shul*. But when we got to *Shul* she wasn't there, which was odd because she had left before we did. Thinking she may have stopped off to buy a packet of cigarettes or something, I made my way to my seat next to Daphne, with Angela's seat on the other side still empty. The service started around 6pm, but there was still no sign of her. By 6.15pm, I was crying. Where *was* she? Then at around

6.30pm – an hour after we had left the house – she arrived, took her seat next to me and never said a word about where she had been. She was smiling like nothing was wrong, and there I was crying away. I was so relieved to see her that I just hugged her. It wasn't the time or place to get into a conversation about where she had gone to, so I decided I would ask her after the service. As it transpired, her reasoning was that she had promised her dad and Felicité she would swing past their house before 6pm. But that made no sense to me at all because when we left, she said she'd see me in a few minutes.

I couldn't sleep the whole night, tossing and turning and worrying about where she had gone. In *Shul* the next day I asked Hymie if Angela had been with them on *Kol Nidre* evening, and he said no. She had promised to come past, he said, but never showed up.

So where the hell had she been?

I phoned Hymie the following week.

'Woosh (after all these years I still called him that), are you sure she wasn't there, like maybe she was and you just never saw her?' I asked daftly. Was I such a lunatic to even think that such a thing could have happened? She's not invisible – if she was there, he would have seen her.

'Annie, she wasn't here,' he answered sadly.

There was nothing I could do but confront her about not having been at Hymie and Felicité. So I did. And yet again she wriggled seamlessly out of it, claiming that her dad had already left for *Shul* and never saw her arrive, but she was there 'for sure'. I could go on and on relating the minutiae of that conversation, which just went around in circles, but what is the point? The fact is that after the no-show at the *Shul*, I think I finally started to accept that Angela had been lying to me at every turn. But I could never prove it. I became obsessed with 'catching her out' but I never could. She was too clever for me. Too clever for all of us.

CHAPTER 6

I can't keep being in denial

Things got undeniably worse in October 2008.

One evening, Lionel and I were sitting in the office. I was trying to remove a bridesmaid from a wedding photo because the bride had had a huge fallout with her soon after the wedding, and wanted her out, gone, removed, deleted like a blight. We photographers can do this – not easily, but it's possible.

Today people want 'guests' added in or taken out. They think it's just one click of the mouse. 'Oh, I can't make the group photoshoot today, so just slot me in with Photoshop, won't you?' So here I was 'de-selecting' the bridesmaid, slowly, carefully, clicking the mouse, pixel by pixel. It had to be perfect...

'Darling, did you by any chance make out a cheque for R1500 and deposit it into your account?'

'Hey?' I turned to Lionel, whizzing around in the chair, leaving the bridesmaid half in and half out the photo.

'Darling, a cheque has been deposited into the account of "A. Brest".'

'Lionel, why would I do that?' I asked, confused. 'And just for the record Angela is also A. Brest.'

Oh. My. G-d. Angela...

I took a closer look at Lionel's bank statement and there it was: 'A.S. Brest.' Angela Shannon Brest.

It was obviously some kind of mistake. It had to be.

But somehow I knew that Angela had something to do with this – how and when and what and where, I couldn't fathom.

I dialled her number immediately, and told her what Lionel had just come out with. She, of course, laughed it off as some mistake. But what mistake? Who would deposit R1500 into Angela's account, if not Angela herself?

But then why would she do that? If she needed money, for any reason, she'd ask me. Wouldn't she? And didn't she just tell me she was 'good' in the money department and didn't need a loan. She had a brilliant job, earned a good salary. Of course she was right – it was some stupid mistake made by the bank.

And yet my mind was churning over and over. Who would take three cheques out of Lionel's cheque book, and deposit one of them into Angela's account? Could it have been one of her friends? There had been a whole crowd of them here a few weeks earlier, so maybe it was one of them? But, again, why would they not deposit the cheque into their *own* account? Maybe it had been Angela's girlfriend? But her girlfriend didn't have her bank account details, or so she said.

I just couldn't make any sense of it, and kept mulling it over and over in my mind. But it remained a mystery, and Lionel and I discussed it over and over and over again. Who would have done this? Who *could* have done this? And why?

And yet none of us did a thing about it, and I didn't say anything to anyone. It plagued me, consumed my thoughts, and although somewhere in the very back of my mind I had a feeling Angela knew more about it than she was letting on, I just couldn't fathom how she was involved. I refused to admit to myself that she may have done it, but there was simply no other explanation. I couldn't bring myself to ask her outright, so I mentioned it in my emails to her: how puzzling it all was, and how worrying, and could it have been one of her friends, and if so, who could it be, did she suspect anyone? And always she'd reply that it was indeed a mystery – but little else. I told her that Lionel suggested we go to the bank and ask for the footage, and she agreed that it was a brilliant idea, and in that way we could get to the bottom of it, and I could put my mind at rest.

'It can't be her,' I insisted to Lionel. 'It just can't.'

'Darling, I'd like to say that I agree with you, but who do you think it was?' he replied as he turned away from the computer to give me his full attention. 'Don't you see that it has to be someone who knows us? Someone who was here, in our office, and yet someone who knows Angela's account details.'

And I agreed. Of course I could see that. I had asked myself the same questions over and over again, always coming up with no answer, at least not one I was ready to believe...

Angela's engaged! She was indeed going to be a bride! Bride to a beautiful young woman. They referred to one another as 'my future wife'. Both were going to wear wedding dresses with veils, and carry bouquets. They were so excited.

The wedding was to be the following year on a wonderful farm in the Cape. As foreign as the idea was to me, of two women getting married – and as little as I understood it – I hugged them both, and offered to not only be at their wedding, but to photograph it for them and make them an album as their wedding gift. I was going with the flow – it was either that, or lose my daughter's love, and that was not an option.

Many Sunday mornings I would go for a walk with my close friend, Daphne Jacks, and one day I confided in her about what was going on at home.

Daphne is very spiritual, logical, emotionally solid, entirely non-judgemental, and I have always respected her knowledge and the way in which she handles difficult situations. Daphne had extraordinary wisdom so when I told her about the mystery of the cheques at home I was hoping she'd say that it was unlikely to be Angela; that it had to be some mistake.

'Annie, that's a tough one... But what does your heart tell you?' she asked as we paced ourselves, walking briskly.

'Daph, I don't know. My heart tells me that she didn't do it. She can't have. She's not like that, Daph.'

'Annie, you *do* know, and I know it's hard to believe, and hard to accept, but you need to look hard at the evidence,' she answered as we turned the corner from Edward Rubinstein Drive into Marion Road.

Daphne is a fast walker and I was trotting along next to her just to keep up. But I enjoyed walking, and the harder I walked the clearer my mind became. Maybe Daphne was right in that I did know the truth, but I couldn't believe that Angela would have been so devious.

And then I told my wise friend Carol Zimmerman, who had known Angela since she was a child. Carol just looked at me, and her face said it all. She shook her head slowly.

So neither Daphne nor Carol could reassure me that I was imagining it. In fact, both let me know loud and clear that they believed Angela was guilty. There was no other logical conclusion. I had to get real.

I knew I needed to tell Robert and Sharon. Somehow, by not telling them, it was easier to pretend that none of this was happening, that I could hide from it, put it aside for another time, deal with it later – just not now. But if I told Robert and Sharon, I would be compelled to confront it, that it would become real. Both my brother and sister-in-law were sensible, solid citizens, and I knew that the time had come to tell them.

We met for coffee at Melrose Arch, and I came right out with it. I told them about Hymie's call, about Lionel's cheque. To say that they were upset is an understatement. They were upset for Ma, for me, and for Lionel.

'So what do you think?' I asked. 'Could there be some other explanation?'

'Anne, come on! What other explanation could there be?' Robert said. The only explanation was staring my brother and sister-in-law in the face, and it should have been staring me in the face all along. So why was I so blind, so unable to see the obvious?

So, with a renewed sense of determination after the meeting with Robert and Sharon, I called Angela and asked her once again if she knew anything at all about the missing cheques.

'No, Mommy,' she actually laughed.

And, once again, I felt awful. My maternal instinct asked how I could even *think* that she would take money from us. But how could Daphne and Carol and Robert and Sharon all be wrong? She had to have taken it. There was simply no other explanation. I knew I had to face the obvious. I can't believe how long it took me to finally accept that Angela was the one taking our money, the one who had taken Lionel's cheque and cashed it. Nobody else could have done it, but her.

But instead of dealing with it there and then, the months slipped away and I did nothing. Angela continued to come to us for *Shabbos* meals.

She was bright company at the table, chatting mainly to Ma, but not much to me, and she didn't even cast Lionel as much as a backward glance. She always had lots to say for herself, but sometimes her fiancée would be quiet, pensive, somewhat detached from the conversation. I put it down to the fact that she felt uncomfortable, maybe because it was hard for her to be with all of us on Friday nights. She was a quiet young woman, a fine musician who was starting to make a name for herself in Johannesburg. I sometimes went to hear her sing, took photographs.

It was clear that she and Angela adored one another. Often they sat holding hands and I had learned to accept it as the norm. But sometimes she did it when Ma was in the room, and I prayed she wouldn't turn around and see it. I knew it would upset Ma terribly. Of course, I should have said something to Angela, suggested some discretion, but I was afraid to rock the boat, afraid Angela would no longer come on a Friday night – and Friday night was the one time that we all had together as a family.

Then in about June 2009 she rocked up at the house to tell me she has just left her wonderful job – suddenly, out of the blue, explaining that she simply needed to 'move on'. And she was upbeat about it.

'Don't worry, Mom, there are loads of jobs out there,' she reassured me.

But were there? Jobs were hard to find these days, and I wondered why she hadn't waited to find another one before she left. She hadn't mentioned anything about leaving before and now, all of a sudden, the job was history. Her fiancée was not thrilled about it either.

My mind went into overdrive. Why would she leave her job? She couldn't afford it – and here she was, convinced she would get another one without too much difficulty, that she'd be snatched up, headhunted, and the old job would become a distant memory.

The uncertainty kept me awake at nights, but I stopped myself from calling her boss. I didn't want to go snooping around behind her back. And if Angela ever found out, she would go mad and I certainly didn't want to get on the wrong side of her, that's for sure.

Then one day soon after the job bombshell, Ma told me that her traveller's cheques were missing from a drawer in her office, as well as some pounds sterling. Gone, just like that... She was nervous. Who would have taken them, who *could* have? No one had a key to her place other than Angela and myself. She was sick over it, not knowing what to think. Of course, it couldn't have been me and it couldn't have been Angela and she trusted her char implicitly. She did neverthless question the char, who said she knew nothing about it – in fact, she didn't even know what a traveller's cheque was. It was a mystery. A first for Ma, but sadly not a first for me.

I had become all too used to these unexplained mysteries, for which there were never any satisfactory answers. Angela ducked and dived and weaved her way in and out of lies and deceit. Nothing was making any sense at all.

And then we discovered that the cheques had been cashed. In Rosebank. Ma had done a bit of detective work on her own, working together with the travellers cheque company, and now there was talk of surveillance footage being hauled out.

At the *Shabbos* table on Friday night, Ma was clearly upset about it all – not so much about the missing cheques themselves, but about who could have taken them, who had had access to her house. She had searched high and low for them, thinking that maybe she had misplaced them, but she knew she hadn't. So what was the answer? They had been taken, that's for sure, and now they had been cashed.

'Gran, there must be footage. Let's find the scum who did this to you,' Angela said, reaching over the table for another slice of mango.

Fiancée was quiet. She was looking down at her hands folded in her lap, saying nothing. My heart skipped a beat. Maybe it was *her* who had taken Ma's traveller's cheques? Is that possible? Could she have gone to visit Ma with Angela, and helped herself to the traveller's cheques? Someone did – and it wasn't me! But then Fiancée was often quiet at the table. Wasn't she?

Fortunately, Robert managed to convince Ma to let the issue of the traveller's cheques go, and not follow through on the surveillance footage. We all knew that the stress of it all could be bad for her blood pressure and, mercifully, Ma decided to listen to Robert.

Angela's bride-to-be was a celebrity, a singer, and a darn good one too. She had moved to Johannesburg so she and Angela could be together, and was well on her way to becoming a top recording artist. As a result, the press regularly showed up at their home for interviews and photoshoots, and of course the two of them would appear together in magazines. Photos of the engaged couple, stories about their hopes and dreams for their future. Ma subscribed to one or two of these publications, delivered to her door daily. What the hell was I going to do? How could I let Ma get up in the morning, go to her door and take in the newspapers or a magazine and read about it?

Ever since I had found out that Angela was gay I had been worrying about Ma finding out. What if someone just mentioned it in passing, presuming she knew? The shock would be too much,

I thought. But what if we told her, and she took it so badly that her blood pressure shot up? So I rang Auntie Freda, Ma's sister in Montreal; she had always been my confidante, ever since I was a girl.

'Anne,' she said softly, 'I know my sister, and I know how this will hurt her – she's of a very different generation. You, Robert and Sharon must decide whether to tell her or not, and whatever decision you all make, I will respect.'

Things had now come to a head, and we were being left with very little choice. Now that Angela was getting married, we would have to tell Ma. And Robert and Sharon agreed – there was nothing for it but for Angela to go and tell her, finished and *klaar*.

I was a wreck, and I felt so sorry for Ma. It wasn't fair; somehow, Ma also had hopes and dreams for Angela, her adored grandchild, her 'beauty'. She had dreams of watching her Angela walk down the aisle, to have a husband and children. I knew, too, though, that these dreams were not Ma's to have, and that Angela's life was her own.

So it was that I rang Angela on her cell. She picked up immediately.

'Ang, you have to tell Gran.' Our conversation started off calmly enough, but I could hear the pitch beginning to rise in my voice, my fear and anger taking over. 'And why did you have to make it so public, for G-d's sake?' As much as I tried to keep my voice on an even keel, I couldn't.

'Please understand that this is one thing I am not doing. You can stand on your head – you and you alone are going to have to do this. I am not having Ma find out her granddaughter is gay by reading it in a glossy magazine. There is nothing for it but to go and see Gran and tell her – and that's the bottom line...'

I waited for the retort and, just as I thought she'd put the phone down on me, she spoke up.

'Mommy, I'll go over and see her this evening and I'll tell her,' she said quietly.

And so she went, just as she promised she would. As it turned out, however, she didn't *really* tell her, did she? She babbled on and on, making very little sense, and Ma wasn't entirely sure what she was actually saying. In effect, Angela made a total mess of it. When I called her to ask how it had gone, she explained that she hadn't really been able to tell Ma anything. She just couldn't do it, she said. And would I?

Robert wasn't happy when he phoned later for an update.

'But, Rob, what can I do? She just couldn't tell Ma. What do you want me to do?'

'Then *you* tell her, Anne.'

So the next morning I went around to Ma's house at 6am to catch the papers and the magazine before Ma found them. I felt like a criminal, turning off the car engine and coasting into the driveway. I slipped out of the car, ducked up the path and grabbed the mail off her porch. Then I snuck back to the car and drove off. She called me later in the morning and mentioned that the mail had not been delivered and she would have to get the newspaper from one of the neighbours.

'Hang on, Ma, I'm coming over now.'

I drove up ten minutes later. She opened the door, happy to have me around in the morning.

'Shall I make you something to drink?' she asked, her voice soft and kind as she closed the door behind us.

'No, Ma. Thanks.'

We sat down, and I spilled the beans.

She took it badly – very badly. *Why, why, why?* She was a woman of almost 90, from a different generation entirely, and it was beyond her powers of comprehension that two women – or two men, for that matter – would want to get married. But Ma is a lady, elegant and poised, gentle and wise, so she accepted what had been dumped in her lap, albeit with great sadness – and a load of endless questions that served only to irritate me.

I did not handle the situation the way I should have, and could have. I got annoyed with her. I heard myself going on and on about the fact that she has five wonderful grandchildren. And that I would probably never have grandchildren from my daughter and if anyone had to be sad, it was *me*. I heard my voice rising, but

49

Ma sat quietly and said nothing. I was annoyed – annoyed that everything had to be this way, that I had had to keep Angela's gay lifestyle from her gran all these years, constantly worrying that someone somewhere would reveal our little secret.

I told Ma about Angela's plans for her future, careful not to use the terms 'fiancée' or 'wedding'. I ranted on about them wanting to have a little ceremony to cement their relationship, but I could see that Ma was struggling to take it in, to understand. She couldn't make head or tail of any of it. All she could do was accept it. What else could she do? What else could anyone do?

And all the while I could not stop shouting. I hated myself for it.

'Why did you not bloody well tell her yourself?' I shouted at Angela on the phone later. 'You're not a child any more, you're an adult. It wasn't my place to tell her, it's yours. It's high time you took responsibility for your own actions.'

I could feel my blood boiling for having visited this on Ma.

'And,' I continued without backing off, 'while I'm about it – why did you have to have all this publicity anyway? Surely you realised that a photoshoot would end up in the magazines? What did you think you were doing? You knew Gran didn't know you were gay – why did you leave it till the bloody last minute to tell her?'

'Mommy, stop making a mountain out of a molehill,' she retaliated. 'It's not a train smash. Gran knows now, so it's all good.'

Friends who tried to make me feel better would comfort me with, 'It's nothing to be gay today' and 'So many people are "coming out"' and 'As long as she's healthy' and 'As long as she's happy'. What else could they say? What else could anyone say? I knew all that. Of course I thanked G-d that she had her health, and that she was happy. It wasn't even the fact that she is gay that upset me, it was what 'being gay' actually meant, and meant for *me*. No son-in-law, no babies, no *machutonim*. It was very difficult to grasp that none of this was about me, it was about *her*, Angela. And if this was how it was to be, then so be it. Finished and *klaar*.

CHAPTER 7

Money, money, money

'There is no way it's Ang, no way at all.'

That's what my son Greg said when he came home for his yearly visit in 2009. He had been living in the USA for much of the last decade, and while BBM and Skyping was the way we kept in constant touch, there was nothing better than seeing him face to face. He had heard about all the bizarre happenings, about the missing money and also household items, and he simply refused to believe his sister was the culprit.

Greg's visit was filled with family get-togethers, family braais, and after each visit, each get-together, money was missing. From all of us. Never huge amounts, but enough to notice…

'Mom, I hate to say this to you,' Greg said one afternoon when we were sitting out in the garden, 'but I'm missing some dollars from my wallet.'

'I don't know what to say, Greg. I just don't know any more.'

As much as I knew she loved her brother, and missed him terribly, Angela had felt abandoned when he left to settle in the USA. I also knew that she resented so much about his visits home. She complained that I always went into shopping overdrive, and bitched about the fridge bursting with all his favourite foods. She would dig at me about how the house was being cleaned from top to toe, how I would always make him 'feather steaks' and spaghetti bolognaise and his favourite cottage pie. I knew she resented the fuss we made over him, and how I would start counting the months, weeks and days until his plane touched down at OR Tambo. She called it the 'big countdown'.

Greg always came laden with gifts. He loves the family, and has a heart of pure gold. He also has a short fuse, which Angela always took great delight in reminding me of. The extended family adored Greg; he was charming and charismatic, and it was hard for me to try to downplay my excitement at his home-coming. She also resented the endless round of parties, *Shabbos* dinners, and braais held in his honour, and she ducked out of most of them. I tried to explain to her that if Gregory lived in South Africa, and she lived overseas, it would be her who would having feather steaks and cottage pie cooked for her, and I know in my heart of hearts that she knew I loved both my children the same, no one child more than the other. If anything, I have loved her longer, because she is my firstborn, and special daughter.

Then my brother and sister-in-law revealed two other incidents I had been entirely unaware of; both my nephews were missing money, and indeed Angela had been in their respective homes on the days the money disappeared. Jesus, what *next*? Stealing money from her cousins? I could see it pained Robert and Sharon to tell me, but they had to, and I was pleased that they did, even though it was so hard for me to hear.

Was she not afraid? What if someone had walked into the room as she was helping herself to their money? G-d Almighty, what would be next? What were we going to do about it? This was not going to simply go away. But still, with all the glaring evidence, I was not convinced it was Angela, despite everything. I started to imagine the wildest of wild scenarios. Maybe Lionel himself deposited the cheque that had gone missing into her account to make it look bad for her, because there was no love lost between the two of them. But was I *crazy*? Lionel would never do that. He was not like that – and yet the idea did cross my mind, the same way that it did when I thought maybe *I* had taken the cheque and deposited it into her account.

But then what about the R2000 that disappeared from his jacket pocket? I remember the night well… He came home, left his jacket on the chair in the room we both used as our office, and thought nothing more of it. The following day he went to work, called home around 9am to tell me that he had brought home R2500 in his jacket pocket and now there was just R500. And would Helen and I please have a look for it. Look for it where? I told him straight out that it was a waste of time looking for it because there was no R2000 lying around the house.

He came home that night in a foul mood.

'Nice that a person can't even leave money in this house for five minutes without it being gone,' he said, spoiling for an argument.

Of course, I had a feeling that Angela had helped herself to the R2000, but instead of feeling contrite and saying I was sorry – which is what I should have done – I shouted at him.

'How many times have I told you not to leave money lying around?' I said, my voice getting louder and higher as I struggled to keep it normal. I tried not to sound confrontational; after all, he was the one missing the money this time, not me.

Then the shouting started and we both lost the plot – arguing about things that had happened a good many years ago, which had nothing to do with the missing money. That is how it always ended. We were always arguing about the situation at home.

When we argued, which was often, he accused me of always defending Angela. And I always retaliated with he was picking on her. I would stay up late at night, on the computer, not wanting to go to bed, my thoughts in turmoil. What was wrong with me? I had more than a gut feeling she was taking the money, so why was I defending her, and fighting with Lionel? He is a good man, and he worked hard for his money, and if it had been the other way around, I would have been furious had one of his children taken money from me. I would have insisted *he* pay it back! But Lionel is not like that. He has a good heart and he felt for me, loved me,

I know he did, but the situation was spiralling well out of control, and I knew that I wasn't supporting him the way I should, But then Angela *is* my daughter.

This is how the family dynamics were moving, and we all started to get a little crazy – and yet always appear normal in front of Ma.

One day I was in the studio waiting for my next client to arrive when the doorbell rang. I opened the door to a man at the front gate asking if I was 'A Brest'. I said I was. He said he had a Writ of Execution to attach my property. He showed me a form, which I could see was a genuine legal document, because I worked for lawyers way back in the mid-sixties. And I knew only too well what a Writ of Execution was, but what I didn't know is why the Sheriff of the Court was serving one on me. I don't owe anyone a dime, so what the hell was all this about?

I refused to open the gate and, naturally, he got belligerent, reminding me he had the power to move his men in and take half my home out with them, if he so chose. I was shaking. But suddenly my mind clicked into place and I told him that there was another 'A Brest'.

'I'm Anne Brest,' I said. 'Which A Brest are you looking for?' By now I was more than a little anxious about what I suspected his answer would be. He glanced down at the form.

'No, Angela Brest. Not Anne.'

Relief poured over me as I realised it wasn't me he was after, but I was devastated that it was Angela, that things were so out of control that we had arrived at this point... I explained to him that Angela didn't live here, none of her things were here. He finally drove off with an apology.

I was still shaking, my heart thumping in my chest. I felt light-headed, as I dialled her number on my cell phone.

'What the fuck's going on? Do you know what just bloody happened?' I screeched, the phone shaking in my hand, my heart still thumping. I was shouting, forgetting how my friend Daphne always told me to try to keep my voice at a regular pitch, to be in control of myself and my emotions. Well, to hell with that! I was in a fury, scared out of my wits – and ashamed.

While not laughing it off exactly, Angela dismissed the entire incident as a 'mistake with admin' and proceeded to reassure me that she didn't owe anyone a cent. She was totally in the clear, she said. So it was all good. And, as unbelievable as it may seem now, I decided to believe her. It was easier somehow, and my daughter was so good at acting innocent.

But that was to be the first of many similar interactions with people looking for Angela, people she owed money. Often, and at inopportune moments, there would be calls from the bank, creditors, service providers, all looking for her. Sometimes people would phone and ask for her and when I explained I was her mom, they'd hang up. There would also be calls from rather dubious characters. I was constantly having to pass messages on, but she never returned the calls, never seemed to open her mail. She was always unavailable – in fact, I often struggled to get hold of her myself. She was forever losing her cell phone, or claiming that it was broken, constantly switching sim cards from one phone to the next.

And she always protested – those big brown eyes staring at me – that she had no idea why anyone would be looking for her, as she was 'in the green'. Apparently, she had no idea what the fuss was about. What was I so upset about, and why was I always nagging her about the fact that the banks were looking for her?

'It's all good, Mommy,' she told me time and time again.

Of course, I desperately wanted to believe her, but then why was I getting an average of two calls a week from people looking for her?

One Friday, around midday, I was at the computer rushing to get some work finished for a client, when she called to tell me that they were off to the Drakensberg for a few days and would I mind lending her some money as she was expecting some money to be put into her account but it hadn't yet showed up. I said I would make the deposit into her bank account so that it would be available as soon as she got to the Drakensberg.

'Mommy, can you not put it in now? We need it before 2pm.'

'Because?' I asked her, annoyed now. She was interrupting my creative flow and, once again, it was about money.

'Because we don't have money for the petrol,' she answered back like I was not seeing the obvious.

The kicker was that she didn't want me to put it into her regular bank account as she was overdrawn and it would have simply been swallowed up, but of course she didn't dare say so. Instead, she said she didn't have the time to come over so asked whether I could go with her to the ATM and I could give her the cash. And so it was that I had to *schlep* after her.

I came home exhausted. She had manipulated me once again, and I had allowed it. I was furious. So I called her. I wanted – needed – to say to her that if they didn't have two cents between them, how could they afford to go on holiday? People who don't have money can't go away just like that. Who was paying for the accommodation at the Drakensberg? It's not cheap there. Oh, she had the answer quick as a flash: they were staying with friends who had a six-bed apartment. And she wasn't broke; it's just that her salary hadn't cleared in her account yet. Once again, she was confusing me, doing my head in.

I can't stand owing money. I have a 'thing' about it. In fact, it's more than a 'thing', it's an obsession. It brings back memories of how Da was always in debt in Ireland, memories accompanied by bouts of nausea and a sense of foreboding. The constant un-certainty, the nightmares, the nausea, the craving for chocolate, and feeling of inferiority when I was with wealthy children.

After the fire in Da's South Anne Street shop, things were very difficult for us. There was just no money. I remember he would give me 2/6d to go and buy his cigarettes (funny that there was always money for those…). 'And before you come home, please go and see Mr Haitch, and ask him if he has a "message" for me.'

So I asked Mr Haitch if he had a message for Da.

'No, lovey,' he said, cigar smoke swirling around his face. I did not like Mr Haitch. He was fat and uncouth, a rotten tooth in the front of his big fat face, and he was always sweaty. Sweaty forehead and sweaty, fat hands.

'Tell your daddy I'll have a message for him on Friday,' he coughed as he spoke.

When I got home and I told Da that Mr Haitch didn't have a 'message' for him but I was to go on Friday, Da said nothing, but I saw he looked over at Ma as he lit up another cigarette. Da smoked non-stop, day in, day out, hour in, hour out. He was never without a cigarette in his mouth.

But Mr Haitch didn't have a 'message' on Friday, nor on the next Friday and I hated having to ask him. I hated watching his piggy eyes and his hot, sweaty face, and his cigar smoke wafting up into his nostrils, his eyes.

That day Da went wild. He slammed his fist on the dining-room table. Robert was playing monopoly on the floor with Anne-Marie from next door, and Da started shouting. He was yelling about Mr Haitch being a bloody *Peruvian* and a bloody *mamser* and he might just as well be stealing food out of our mouths by not sending the 'message'. Da was in a rage.

'Children, go out and play for a while, your daddy's not feeling well.'

Because Mr Haitch hadn't sent Da the 'message' – which I later learned was the £25 he owed him for a pair of glasses, and £20 for a pair for his wife – Da couldn't pay Walsh's chemist bill that month. When you're a child, you hear your parents talking, and what you hear penetrates the subconscious. You may not fully understand, but yet you know it's not good. And what I heard made me knot-in-my-stomach nauseous. Mr Walsh supplied Da with his nerve tablets, even though Da sometimes paid him only a few months later.

Da had been promising to pay Mr Walsh's bill but Mr Haitch had put paid to that. Ma and I had to cross over the Harold's Cross Road one day so as not to have to see Mr Walsh if he came out of the shop. I remember that it gave me a terrible feeling in the pit of my stomach, and I hated Mr Haitch for this.

Besides, Mr Haitch was rich. Their house had thick carpets; it was warm. They had beautiful ornaments everywhere, little figurines with stiff-netted dresses, musical boxes that played a tinkling tune when you opened them. There were gorgeous lace curtains and thick outer curtains in a thick red velvet, with gold corded ties to hold them back in the daytime. They had a lovely car too – and Da never had a car.

Why couldn't he have just given Da the money? Why did he drive Da to distraction for months. It affected Da and it affected all of us, and I remember Da shouting in rage, and how he would bang his fist on the dining-room table in raw anger and frustration. Da was down on his luck, and Mr Haitch knew this; there wasn't a soul in Dublin who hadn't heard about the fire in the shop, and how Da lost everything, including his peace of mind and his dignity.

And today, as much as I have a fear of ever owing anyone money, and a blind obsession to pay my accounts in advance, I also don't like anyone to owe me. Patterns repeat themselves, and when I first started my own photographic studio, I remember how people would come to collect their photos when I was out on a shoot, and say to Helen: 'Tell the Madam I'll pay her next time.'

'Tell the Madam I forgot my chequebook.'

'The Madam knows me, it's okay.'

'Tell the Madam I'm not leaving the country.'

'Tell the Madam I'm good for the money.'

And then the wait would begin. They were busy, they were away, they had problems, issues, they were sick, the dog was sick, the maid was sick, they were 'hectic', and all this time I would be desperate for the money they owed me. R200 went a long away in 1982. But that's what people would do. Would they have gone to Edgars without a chequebook? Or claim to have left their chequebook in the car? Would they tell Pick n Pay that their dog is sick and they have to run to the vet and they would pay for their groceries later? Would they tell Stuttafords that they are not leaving the country and they are good for the money? They wouldn't even get a roll of toilet paper without paying for it, and that is how it should be. You buy something, you pay for it, right there and then. I think it's a sin to make people wait for their money particularly if you can well afford it.

A photographer I know made a sign – one for his studio, and one for mine – that stated: 'Just because you know me doesn't mean you don't have to pay me.'

Even today, I'm fastidious about paying my debit long before the statements arrive. I can't bear thinking I owe anyone anything. And it made me anxious and sick to the stomach to even think that Angela was in debt. So with Angela's endless money stories now becoming an almost daily occurrence, out of the blue I got an idea. I decided that to hell with everything, I was going to phone Angela's ex-boss. I was put through straight away and I asked her outright, 'Why did Angela leave her job?' Out with it, just like that. I must have caught her off-guard…

'I wish you hadn't asked me that question,' she said very quietly into the phone.

CHAPTER 8

The hand in the cookie jar

Shattered.

Oh G-d, I could barely breathe.

I had asked, opened the bee box and now I had the answer. But what I heard, never in my wildest late-night sleepless, dreamless moments, had I imagined.

It was a very long story, one of underhandedness, lies, deceit, of lie detector tests, and large sums of money that had gone missing. A story of her fellow colleagues' credit cards being used fraudulently, large sums of money – including R60 000 in cash – having disappeared, of office cupboards being broken into, and stories of Angela in the bathroom with little packets of white powder that her colleagues described as cocaine...

Oh G-d, was that what all of this was about? Drugs? Cocaine? *Cocaine?* My heart was thumping, my mouth dry, I could hardly breathe. I was hyperventilating, couldn't get enough air into my lungs. This couldn't be real, I was dreaming. I needed to wake up – and fast.

But it was real. Very real. I knew I had to deal with it, confront her once and for all. I didn't give a shit. I knew she'd be furious with me for daring to phone her boss, but this had been the last straw. And I wasn't going to take it any more. I was sick and tired of pussy footing around her, putting up with her lies and her crap, and I was not going to tread carefully around her one more day, not one more hour, nor one more second. I was livid. I felt deceived, betrayed, cheated, embarrassed and lied to.

Before I could backtrack on my newfound bravado, I called her and told her I wanted to see her. I had plucked up the courage of my convictions, courage I should have had and used all these months. She started to tell me all the things she had to do, that her car was not going very well – but I simply cut her off.

'I don't care how you get here, just get here, and hurry the fuck up.'

I heard her key in the door 25 minutes later. She was hardly in the door when I started in on her. I told her that I'd rung her boss and I knew about the missing money, the credit-card fraud, the R60 000 missing from the cupboard, the foreign currency all gone, the cocaine in the bathroom, and everything else. She glared at me, her gorgeous eyes incredulous…

I saw her lips tighten, a flash in her eyes, her determination.

'Mom, let's go right now. Let's go to the company and get this sorted. Right away.'

She was so brazen, so confident, so 'not bothered' by what I was saying that I immediately began to doubt myself, started to wonder if her boss had lied to me, made it all up.

'I left,' she continued, almost patronisingly, 'because I was so tired of having to work at nights. And it was hard for my fiancée too – she couldn't handle the long nights alone, and I just decided to put her first and quit my job, that's all.' She laughed lightheartedly, a smile playing on her lips. As if she was relieved that she had passed the test.

But this time I was relentless. I couldn't let her manipulate me this time.

'And what's this about you having cocaine in the bathroom at work?' I yelled. 'You were seen sniffing in there – is that what you are? A bloody drug addict?' I spat it out, my throat raspy from shouting…

'Mommy, I swear to you, I wouldn't touch cocaine, ever,' she said. 'And why would you believe my boss over me?'

'And the lie-detector tests – how come you never bloody well mentioned that you had lie-detector tests done at work, and that you failed one of them? Why?'

'Mommy, lie-detector tests aren't always accurate – they're not even admissible in court.'

'But how come you never even mentioned it?' I wasn't giving up. I knew I was harassing her, but I was beyond caring.

'Sorry, Mommy, I would have, but I just didn't think it was important.'

She always had answers. But this time I wasn't buying it. I'd reached my own point of no return. She was stealing and lying and something had to be done. I had to do something or I would have been as guilty as she was. I knew I was part of the problem, that I had chosen to stay blinkered for so long, guilty for not dealing with this whole miserable situation properly from the start. It had crept up on us all so slowly that by the time I finally started to actually *do* something about it, a few years had gone by.

In the end she left, still insisting on her innocence, insisting that everyone else was wrong. I had failed to get through to her.

I wrote her an email the following day, pouring out my heart, asking her why all these bizarre things kept happening, why it was that so many of her friends were missing money – her fiancée herself had money missing, a lot of it, and one of her sisters had an issue with her over a credit-card spending spree. Summonses had arrived for her, and even once when I was in America with Gregory, I was woken up one night by a text message telling me that unless I paid the outstanding balance to some doctor, legal action would be taken against me. Against *me*? I didn't even know the doctor, had never heard of him. I had called from Los Angeles to South Africa first thing in the morning, and it turned out they had got it wrong. The message had been for Angela, not for me.

I listed all these examples, questioned her about everything I could remember. I explained how I was reaching the end of my rope, that I was spinning around in circles. I brought up the whole conversation I had had with her boss and asked why on earth her boss would have told me all of this if it had not been true. I said I was done with being a sucker. Something had to be done, the dance of madness had to be stopped and I was not putting up with any of her lies for one more second.

She never got the email. But ultimately that might have been the best thing that ever happened. It was divine intervention stepping in. It was her fiancée who got the email instead. She phoned me almost immediately. I thought she was going to blast my head right off for sending Angela such an angry letter, but she simply burst into tears. Tears of pain, tears of relief, tears because she told me that she thought *she* was going mad, and that everything I was experiencing, she was too. Her tears did not stop, because now she knew the truth.

It all came rushing out then, and through her sobs, her pain and her anguish, she told me that she was missing a lot of money, that her credit card had been abused. She said that cash was also disappearing, and that Angela had traveller's cheques – traveller's cheques that Ma was missing – she claimed her gran had given her as a gift. That Friday night, all those months ago when Ma had spoken about her missing traveller's cheques at the table, the truth had hit her like a hammer to the head. But she had been unable to say anything at the time. Like me, she had preferred to believe there must have been some kind of misunderstanding, some mistake. Angela had managed to con and manipulate all of us.

That day, when the truth was finally on the table, her fiancée and I spoke for hours, comparing details – and her stories were all the same as mine. Until now neither of us had known what Angela had been doing with the money.

But now we did.

Drugs.

That was it. Of course. How could we all have been so blind? So stupid?

Fiancée then told me that Angela would disappear for hours on end, but always had a very logical explanation for her disappearances.

Then she dropped another bombshell. She told me that she could not spend another night under the same roof as Angela; she needed time to think, to sort her head out. Can't say I blamed her. At that point I almost wished I could do the same. But, of course, she was my daughter. How could I even think that!

That night Angela arrived home in a heap, sat on the floor in my office, broken, spent, confused, devastated, angry, and torn apart by grief. It was as though for the first time the truth had finally sunken in.

She spent the night in her old bedroom, and most of the next day lying on her bed watching TV. She wouldn't come out of her room. She was demented with grief and pain. All she wanted was for Fiancée to come and get her, and make it all go away, and carry on her life, as though nothing had happened. But Fiancée was having none of it. None of it.

We met up the next day. She gave me bags of Angela's clothes, and made it quite clear that she didn't want her back in the house. I begged her to take Angela home, and tried to reassure her that whatever the drug problem was, we'd help her. But she had made up her mind. She felt so betrayed. She talked to me of broken hopes, broken dreams and broken trust.

How could Angela have done this to her? She tried to explain how much she loved Angela, and thought Ang loved her too, but how could anyone love someone and still do to them what Ang had done to her?

She told me how they had fired the maid for stealing cash from the house, when it was Angela all along... How could Angela have allowed that to happen?

How indeed?

Everything was now such a muddle in my head. That's what lies do to you. I could no longer remember the sequence of events, when I first started suspecting something was wrong, and how long it had been going on. How long had we been walking around, while she was stealing from right under our noses? I started to scratch through my files, files of where she had done copy-and-paste jobs on the figures on her bank statements, statements she had to produce to Fiancée to show that she had paid bills, when, in fact, she hadn't paid them at all. Files where I kept notes Angela had scribbled to me, where I recorded certain pieces of information, some of the accounts I had photocopied – files I kept because I had long stopped trusting my own memory. I felt like such a fool.

In the end, though, as hard as these relentless truths were – and as they all came screaming to the fore at once – in the greater scheme of things, at least the veil had been lifted, at least we knew now without a shadow of a doubt that something was terribly wrong.

CHAPTER 9

Heart attack

That same night, the night that Angela moved back home after Fiancée chucked her out, the night of 3 December 2009, Lionel had a heart attack. A near-fatal one, right there while he was sitting on the couch talking to me. Within seven minutes my paramedic nephew Gavin was there, followed by *Hatzolah* – a Jewish emergency medical service – and an ambulance, and after Gavin did some customary tests, Lionel was hauled off to a clinic virtually on his last legs. He was crying, shouting to me to follow the ambulance, so I ran back into the house to get the car keys and follow.

The timing could not have been worse. A quadruple bypass was soon to follow. I was distraught. Totally. I never saw it coming.

Then the old Angela seemed to spring back from almost out of nowhere. She kicked in almost immediately and got herself up, out of her sorry state. Old Angela, my gentle, kind, caring daughter took charge. She rushed me to the clinic and while she herself didn't visit him, she waited for me for two hours and drove me home again.

She could see that I was in shock and totally shattered. I was a mess. I remember that she made me a cup of boiling hot sugar water, and we sat up chatting till late. Not just about the heart attack, and not just about her situation, but just chatting – like we used to, looking through some of our photograph albums, happier times, photos of her with her arms around her brother, sitting on the beach in Umhlanga with Granny, school photos, birthday parties. It was like a dream.

Of course it didn't last, and in the days that followed the other Angela returned. She spent her days mooching around in the garden, sitting in the chaise, smoking, lying in bed for hours on end, lazing in the sun moping. She appeared to be in a bad emotional state.

Nothing further was mentioned about the stealing, the money, or the drugs. A wall seemed to have been built, one that came up overnight. All she wanted was to have Fiancée back in her life, and nothing else mattered.

I felt so helpless. I was her mother, yet there didn't seem to be a thing I could do for her.

A few weeks later, in late December 2009, at my wits end, I took her to see Gaye Turiel, a friend from years back, who was part of Houghton House Recovery Centre at that time, and who I knew to be a highly successful drug counsellor. There were urine tests, questions, questionnaires, but they found nothing suspicious beyond a trace of Thinz diet pills in her urine. They did, however, suggest that she join an outpatient programme with First Step, a recovery centre with a Twelve-Step programme that meant a 4pm to 7pm meeting every night. I must say I was surprised she agreed. Off she went. Quiet as a lamb, no fuss, no bother. I could hardly believe it.

But once she got there she denied using drugs, denied using cocaine.

'But why are you agreeing to go to First Step, if you are not addicted to drugs?' I asked her.

And the answer came back at me quick as a flash...

'Just to get you and everyone else off my back.'

'Well,' I said, 'if I wasn't using drugs, there's no way I'd allow myself to go to rehab just to get people off my back.'

'Ja, but you're not me, Mom.'

And that was it. Angela was adamant that there was no drug problem.

She offered absolutely no explanation for all the missing money. And when I asked about it, she would shrug her shoulders, that her guess was as good as anyone's. How would she know where all the money went? It had nothing to do with her at all. It was just sheer coincidence that everyone in the family had noticed the same thing: that when Angela was around, money disappeared.

'Not my problem,' she would say.

And, as they say, life goes on – and it did. Looking back now it seems insane that I could just have accepted her bad reasoning and excuses. Maybe I was too tired, too caught up with life and Lionel's health to really interrogate her.

I was running to the hospital twice a day, to see Lionel who had since been admitted to Johannesburg General for his quadruple bypass, running my photography business, seeing to the dogs, shopping, tending my vegetable garden and running to Pretoria (I am also a family historian/researcher and spend a lot of time at the National Archives there as well as at the infuriating Home Affairs Office).

Perhaps I had no time (or real inclination) to dig and dig for the truth; perhaps I preferred to believe that my precious child was many things but not a dirty, scaly drug addict.

The one thing that was blatantly clear, though, was that Angela was now in more debt than ever. She owed everyone around her: her cell phone service provider, various banks, car payments, credit cards. Everything was hopelessly in arrears.

Thank G-d for Robert (and Hymie, too, actually) who now came to the party with financial help. They saw to the 'numbers', as Lionel put it, and I set up a programme in Excel where I paid her creditors each month. It had to be done, to be taken care of, each and every month, because she was not working, and so not earning – and didn't seem to care one way or another as long as everyone stayed off her back. And as long as she had cigarettes. She was smoking like she was on a mission, tossing the butts all over the garden, into the nasturtiums, the geraniums, the alyssum, my roses, and in the flowerpots. I wanted to go mad but stayed cool and eventually handed her an empty honey jar and asked her to place her cigarette butts into that. The jar was filled in a matter of days, but she would never empty it into the rubbish bin. So I did.

Despite the jar, there were still butts outside the front door, in the courtyard, in the driveway. One day Ma visited and she admired the vegetable garden, the lettuces, and marvelled at how healthy everything was looking. I beamed with pride. I loved it when Ma gave me praise, and I worked hard in the little garden, always busily feeding the soil with our own home-grown compost, and pulling out weeds, pruning, feeding the plants, and getting rid of the snails. Then I saw the full jar of cigarette butts next to the tomato plants, staring us both in the face. Ma didn't know that Angela smoked, and hadn't noticed the jar, so I nipped in between Ma and the honey jar and managed to kick it sideways under the yesterday-today-and-tomorrow bush next to the tomatoes.

I wouldn't allow Angela to smoke in the house. It wasn't even up for discussion. I hated the smell of cigarette smoke for one thing, and I didn't want my house reeking of it for another. Angela herself reeked of cigarettes; she brought the smell into the house when she came in from outside, but fortunately for her, Ma didn't have a great sense of smell and had never once noticed the foul smell on her breath.

Ma had actually smoked herself (albeit for a very short time) when she was very young. I saw a cigarette in her hand in a photo taken in the early fifties at some family *simcha* and I had asked her about it. 'It was fashionable,' she had said. 'Everyone smoked.' But Ma said she never, ever smoked in front of her parents. It was just something that young people in her day didn't do. People respected their parents – the Fifth Commandment, 'Honour thy father and thy mother', was taken very seriously. That entire generation had reverence for their parents, respected them, and didn't want to hurt them in any way. Ma still said that nobody would dare smoke in front of their parents even as adults. Smoking was very social, glamorous even, and nobody was aware then of the connection between cigarette smoking and cancer. That had been Ma's world, and the world she and her generation grew up in, the world of my Da and of all my grandparents.

Eventually Angela got a job – not the greatest job, but it was a job nevertheless. Actually it was in photography as an events photographer. She's a good photographer, has a great eye, and I gave her a camera for one of her birthdays. We got some equipment together for her, and she began to shoot quite a few functions.

The money she made didn't go very far, though. Firstly, she had to pay for having her car brakes fixed and she had to catch up the arrears on her cell phone before they cut her off again. Between Hymie, Robert and me, we paid for the First Step programme, which cost a good few thousand smackers for the first month (that included her initial assessment) and then quite a bit less in subsequent months. If my memory serves me correctly, it was around R2000 a month for meetings and therapy sessions – a fair amount of money for us, but we didn't begrudge it at all. It would be money well spent if she cleaned up her act.

I kept her on a very tight leash, which I know she resented, but I just couldn't trust her, and I knew if I gave her more money she would blow it. I gave her R100 for toiletries and cigarettes and demanded the receipt each time. When she needed petrol, I would see to it, but again demanded the slip. There were times when I actually went and bought her cigarettes myself – something I couldn't believe I was doing.

She continued living at home, not thrilled with herself of course, but chipper enough now that she was working. She was pretty much 'over' Fiancée by now, or so she said, and was getting on with her life.

Part of her therapy was to stop being in denial – she had still not admitted that she had used drugs – and to tell her loved ones what had been going down the last few years. But still nothing was said. It was, for her, as though nothing had happened, and life was just going on.

She joined Debt Busters, a company who pay off your bills for you. It can be a long, slow process, depending on how much you can afford to pay them monthly. We paid the monthly instalments. I kept a record on an Excel spreadsheet of every cent coming in and every cent going out.

I would question her about her meetings at First Step, but she shut me up each time, telling me that it was confidential and not to be spoken about. I left it at that. I was simply pleased to see that she seemed interested in the programme – in fact, she even went on a hike with the group and started, very slowly, to look a little healthier.

Ma, however, was asking questions, lots of them: Why was Angela living at home? Why was she not still with 'her friend'? What was going on? Why was she (Ma) so much in the dark?

'I feel like there is a lot I'm not being told,' she said to me one day, pouring herself a strong cup of tea into her china tea cup. Ma wouldn't drink tea out of anything else but a china tea cup, said that was the only way to drink tea.

'Nothing's going on, Ma,' I tried to reassure her. 'Angela's just taking the break-up very badly and decided to live at home for a while.' I lied straight-faced to her. What else was I to say? That Angela had no money, not a great job, had stolen from her workplace and was battling drugs and substance abuse, which she denied anyway?

As much as I loved my daughter, and as happy as I was to have her at home (albeit under disturbing circumstances), it was not an easy time. For example, I had to be careful about where I left my bag. I had started hiding it and sometimes didn't always remember where I had put it, and I had to be careful never to leave even R20 lying around, because I didn't want to put Angela to the test, or put any kind of temptation in her away. It was awful.

Her room was an appalling mess, dirty clothes all over the place, empty cigarette cartons stuffed with butts, crumpled-up petrol slips, splinters of matches, discarded bits of silver paper, endless pairs of denims lying over chairs, on the bed, on the floor and on the door handle. It was one filthy mess. Her personal hygiene had also gone to hell; her fingernails were grimy, and her greasy, unwashed hair was often hidden under a collection of filthy hats the worst of the lot being a vile old velveteen cap.

Something was wrong. I could feel it. Her cell phone was always broken, then a second cell phone of mine went missing (I tore the place apart looking for it), her car was forever breaking down and I always seemed to be trying to organise the money to fix everything rather than risk her being stranded in the middle of nowhere. Money issues again. And strange happenings, unexplained actions. I answered the phone once or twice to a man who asked for her. He wouldn't give a name, but I could hear from his accent that he was West African. I tried to trace the call but couldn't – and of course she knew nothing about it.

Around mid-2010, when she had been attending the Twelve-Step programme for about six months, a friend of hers, Lynda, for whom she had house-sat over Christmas the previous year, called me to tell me she was missing some clothing and would I have a look in Angela's cupboard. I did and I found a few of the items: a designer-label pair of cut-off denims, a black V-neck jersey and a few other miscellaneous items. No biggie, it could have been an innocent mistake. But when I phoned Angela to tell her I'd invited Lynda to come over and collect her things the following weekend, the denims disappeared from sight. I knew I'd seen them, and I knew they had been in the cupboard when I had looked for them – I had seen them with my own two eyes. Was I losing it after all?

Lynda then reminded me that I had described them over the phone. I had even read out the name and the size, so there was no way I could have imagined that. When Lynda came to collect what was hers, I asked her about her cat because when Angela was house sitting for her, she used to ask me for money to feed the cat. I did find that odd because surely Lynda would have left enough cat food? Then Lynda told me she didn't even have a cat!

Lynda had always been a good friend, so she was beyond upset at how Angela's life seemed to be spiralling out of control. She admitted that she was now starting to notice more and more things that had gone missing, things she hadn't even thought of looking for – like her iPod, which was also gone.

Once again that feeling of despair descended on me. I thought it had all gone away, that her problems had been fixed. I mean, what more could I do? She was in therapy, she was with First Step, she lived at home. I didn't know what else to do to stop the madness. I was now neurotic, paranoid, and spent my days blaming myself.

And obviously I was not the only one who blamed me...

Early in 2009 I began writing to Angela's older sister, Sharleen, asking her to meet with me to discuss some of the strange happenings going on around Angela. I knew that Angela had hoodwinked her out of a good bit of money by abusing her credit card, but I also knew that she loved Angela and only wanted what was best for her. I knew Sharleen to have her head screwed on the right way and I wanted to hear from her that 'Yes, Angela has a serious problem.' I needed her reassurance that it wasn't just my paranoia.

Our correspondence started off quite normally and we arranged to meet, but within a very short time, Sharleen got angry with me, furious actually. She slated me for having only spoken to a therapist at the end of October and it was now the end of January 2009. What had I done? Nothing. I had done *nothing*. As far as Sharleen was concerned, I had failed Angela. She said I was not addressing the obvious, that all I do is talk about it to anyone who will listen, and *that*, in her opinion, was 'bloody pathetic'. She was embarrassed that I was doing 'bugger all' about it and warned that it was high time I acted 'as a parent'.

I knew she was right, but it was hard to read. Emails flew backwards and forwards and soon turned nasty. Sharleen was angry with me in her own right, going back to the days of my marriage to her father. And it just seemed to get worse and worse – to the extent that I simply started shoving the print-outs of her emails into drawers. I couldn't face them any more.

She was obviously angry, and dredged up so much history, all typed out in bold, capitals, underlined and highlighted. But through each and every one of Sharleen's horrific emails, I knew that she loved Angela and I knew that I had to do something. What the hell was I waiting for? She was certainly right about that.

On some level I must have known – but chose not to see – that Angela was not coming right, not as clean as she professed to be and, yes, I always seemed to need second opinions from everyone, including Sharleen, who by this stage, had had quite enough of my denial. I suppose she was just sick to death of my blinkered approach. And yet, with her choice use of words, she did manage to get through to me on at least some level, which led to something of a new awakening. But what a ride it was! I got to the stage where I dreaded seeing her name in my Inbox. Oy vey!

Of course, Angela also blamed me. I saw it in the scribblings about her life she had left lying around her pigsty of a room, and I was horrified at how she described me at times. She named me as one of the 'triggers' for her using and blamed me for always being 'on her back'. Said I was 'weak'. I liked to believe that it was her drug-addled state of mind talking, but sadly I knew she had harboured much resentment against me even before using. My problem with all of this was why she had built up so much anger against me, when I had always seen myself as a good mother. Nobody is perfect and mothering is not always easy, but I love both my kids, and gave them every ounce of my being. Years ago she had spat out at me that parents should do a course on parenting before having children. She resented me for 'brainwashing' her with *Torah* beliefs that homosexuality is an 'abomination' – if the truth be told, I had said no such thing. With my greatest respect to our *Torah*, I don't for one moment believe that homosexuality is an abomination. While I enjoy keeping kosher and keeping *Shabbos* to the best of my ability, I have never had a desire, nor do I have the knowledge, to preach from the *Torah*. But yet, there it was in black and white, that I had brainwashed her with Torah beliefs. Where on earth did she get it from? To me, what is an abomination is a husband who cheats on his wife, men who beat their wives, and women who abuse children, the sickos who abuse animals, and all the unspeakable things that go on in this society of ours.

I can well understand a woman loving another woman with her whole soul, or a man loving another man. We are born to love, and how that love is expressed can never be an abomination. For me, as a mother, the sad part of homosexuality is not having grandchildren. But that is my own issue, and something I have to deal with.

Angela also blamed her addiction on the fact that I raised her and Gregory in a religious home, where religious values where 'shoved down her throat'. She resented me for destroying my marriage and breaking up our home. She felt I should never have left her dad, that I should have stayed with him no matter what he did or didn't do, and that divorce was what had brought her to the conclusion that she was 'not good enough', that she had been 'abandoned'. She blamed me for her being neurotic, and believed that I loved Gregory more than I loved her.

But where was this coming from? I was struck by guilt, even shock. Was I the cause of all this? I started to wonder if I had done the right thing in ending my marriage, whether it was wrong to have brought them up in a fairly religious home. Why had I never seen it? At the time, Angela had seemed to love it all; she had loved Friday nights, and going to *Shul*, and all our little traditions. Whatever she said, I understood that I may have had many faults but no one could say my two children weren't my entire world; no one could say I loved one more than the other, ever. So why did she think Gregory was the favourite child?

I discussed what I had discovered reading her notes with her counsellor at the time, but she explained that drug addicts like to pass the buck. They blame others, they blame their home life, their mothers, their fathers, their circumstances, things that happened to them – real or imagined – anything at all, just as long as they don't have to take responsibility for their own actions. I remember a TV programme called *The Dinosaurs* and in one episode, Fran, the mother, had a nightmare in which the baby is an 'adult baby' appearing on some talk show in his nappy promoting a book he had written called, wait for it... *I Blame You, Mommy*. The show was a scream, a total spoof of modern American life.

But even though I wanted to believe it was all a result of Angela's projection, I still lived with my own guilt. I was still reading her mail, trying to piece together what was going on in her life, and the one thing that continued to rear its ugly head was the issue of her debt. To be so broke, she had to still be using, and yet she swore she was clean. In fact, she was diligently counting the months that she was 'clean and serene' – and, besides, I had never seen her stoned, out of it, smashed, trashed, or wasted. If I had, I certainly hadn't recognised it as such.

After she had moved back in, Lionel and her were sharing a bathroom. But in Angela's mind, it was *her* bathroom. She had lived in this house from the age of four, she had grown up here, so it was still hers. She had bathed in the same bath since she was a child, Gregory too, and the medicine cabinet still had things in it that belonged to him. But Lionel saw it as *his* bathroom. He'd used it for the last five years, since we got together, and he resented it when she left anything lying around. She, in turn, resented him being in there, and this caused the most horrendous arguments at home. Sometimes Lionel and I would talk well into the night about it. Sometimes he would be so kind, so understanding, so sympathetic, and caring. He always called me 'darling' and I loved that, but when something else had gone missing yet again, his patience would wear thin, and we'd argue. I'd lie awake all night, unable to sleep, and would wake up in the morning physically and emotionally exhausted.

I felt like I was living in a circus, and that I was the juggler, trying to keep them from each other's throats. I was always tidying up 'their' bathroom so that Lionel wouldn't see the mess and freak out. Because they were seldom on speaking terms, they would send message to each other via me. Not the greatest environment for happy living. On top of it, I had to make sure that Lionel kept calm, because an altercation would have sent his blood pressure soaring.

The very words 'blood pressure' were an unpleasant and scary reminder for me. From when I was little, and my brother and I were being too loud, or arguing, or whatever it was, my Da used to scream, 'Would yiz stop – I feel my blood pressure rising!' Da's blood pressure was always rising, and it was always my fault somehow. I heard it over and over again. I didn't want to be the reason for anyone's blood pressure rising.

In the meanwhile, I watched Angela like a hawk. But what was I looking for? I wouldn't have known the difference between what would be considered normal or a bad acid trip. I never saw (or noticed) her ever looking or behaving differently. This wouldn't be something like being 'drunk' or 'too giggly' or anything. I simply did not know what I was looking for. She continued to go to her meetings at First Step, to Narcotics Anonymous meetings, and whatever else her programme required. She never offered much information, never once apologised for the missing money, or what she had put me through – put us all through. She did say, 'Sorry, Mommy', once, but it didn't cut it somehow. I know they are supposed to apologise to us, and to me, but an apology is not the word 'sorry', it's *being* sorry, and expressing it – saying it means nothing.

Through it all, I tried to ignore all the bad stuff and to be supportive. I tried not to nag. I tried to understand how she could have done it, caused so much trouble and not really ever said she was sorry. I tried to understand what it was about the drugs that made them take such a strong hold of her, how they could take over her value system and entire moral code. Who would have known that me giving her such unconditional support was actually contributing to the problem.

CHAPTER 10

Drug Google

Finally I got a little closer to the truth when I learned that she had been on something called 'CAT'. Besides the definition of 'feline', I had never heard of it. So I had to Google it on the Internet: 'CAT (Methcathinone) is a monoamine alkaloid and psychoactive stimulant similar to cathinone, the primary psychoactive compound in CAT (khat/kat). It is used as a recreational drug and considered to be addictive. It is usually snorted, but can be smoked, injected, or taken orally.' My mind was a blur as I read it over and over again.

But once I started looking I couldn't stop. I got hungry for more and more. The search for answers became my own drug. I often went onto the internet, sometimes in the middle of doing something else. Sometimes at strange hours of the night I would find myself searching, looking for information, trying to put together the missing pieces. I couldn't keep away from the internet, day and night, in between my work assignments, or in between searching for someone's death notice in the Pretoria archives, I would go online and begin searching, looking, more searching. I wanted answers – what was this *CAT* thing?

I couldn't believe what I read. Firstly, drugs contained the most awful ingredients: battery acid, swimming-pool acid, chlorine. Half the time, I didn't even understand what I was reading. I had never heard of some of these words. Then I read something that made my blood run cold... Was this what Angela had been experiencing?

'Chronic use of methcathinone produces a range of problems typical of addiction to powerful stimulant drugs including:

- paranoia and delusions
- hallucinations, including a sensation of bugs crawling under the skin
- anxiety followed by depression
- tremors and convulsions
- anorexia, malnutrition, and weight loss
- sweating, dehydration, and electrolyte imbalance
- stomach pains and nausea
- nose bleeding and eventual destruction of nasal tissues and erosion of the nasal septum
- elevated blood pressure and heart rate
- body aches.'

I read how after a CAT binge, users often report a 'crash' that can include 'severe psychological depression and suicide ideation'.

What the hell was 'suicide ideation'? I rushed to Google – 'having suicide ideas'. How dreadful. Did Angela want to end it all, to die? Was my child a suicide risk? I could hardly breathe.

But still, however much it upset me, I couldn't stop reading. I learned how methcathinone (CAT) is highly addictive, similar to crack cocaine; how some addicts reported developing tolerance and withdrawal symptoms after just one binge of around six to ten days; and how addiction to methcathinone/CAT appears to be just as difficult to treat as addiction to crack cocaine.

Slowly it all began to make horrible sense. Although a lot of it was jargon, words I was unfamiliar with, words I had never heard of, I began to understand what this drug was doing to my daughter.

I read about terms such 'physiological dependence', which occurred when the body has to adjust to the substance by incorporating the substance into its 'normal functioning'. This state creates the conditions of 'tolerance and withdrawal'. Tolerance is the process by which the body continually adapts to the CAT and requires increasingly larger amounts to achieve the original effects.

'Withdrawal' refers to physical and psychological symptoms experienced when reducing or discontinuing a substance on which the body has become dependent. Symptoms of withdrawal generally include anxiety, irritability, intense cravings for the substance, nausea, hallucinations, headaches, cold sweats and the shakes.

These were intricate medical terms, and I honestly didn't understand half of them, and had to read and re-read them until they made some kind of sense.

During these frenetic searches and desperate attempts to understand, I would become furious with Angela. I would think of my friends, proud of their daughters and sons, enjoying time with their adorable grandchildren, and here I was reading about my daughter the addict, trying to make sense of it all, trying to educate myself and trying to understand what Angela was actually putting into her body. Poisoning herself with. I resented her for this and then I would feel guilty for the resentment. It was simply messing with my head.

Why hadn't I seen any of it? Angela didn't seem anxious to me (but then what would I know about the medical definition), but she certainly was aggressive and constantly on the shortest fuse. I now remembered how she was often nauseous, usually starting on a Friday morning, and I knew that a cop-out for our Friday-night family supper was on its way. She would inevitably pass it off as having eaten something 'off' the night before. In terms of cravings, I wouldn't have known, and I hoped she never hallucinated but, again, I wouldn't have known. Tremors and cold sweats? No bloody idea.

There was more. I read that CAT consumption induces mild euphoria and excitement, similar to the effect brought on by strong coffee. According to what I read, individuals under the influence of the drug become very talkative. Slowly I began to recall some of these symptoms in Angela... The manic behaviour and hyperactivity definitely. It was weird but at the time – while it was all playing out right in front of me – I hadn't notice.

I also read how similar in effect it was to those produced

by amphetamine. Amphetamine is a stimulant and an appetite suppressant. It stimulates the central nervous system (nerves and brain) by increasing the amount of certain chemicals in the body. This makes the heart beat faster and raises the blood pressure and decreases appetite. That's why so many young girls like using the drug, because CAT is an effective anorectic (causes loss of appetite). I learned how a lot of them get hooked in their attempt to lose and control weight. I remember how Angela had been on an over-the-counter diet pill called Thinz. Although she was never an overweight child, she was well built, sturdy and stocky, like many in the Brest family. I had supported her when she went about losing weight over a few years; it suited her, she was looking amazing. I was thrilled. Her naturally dark skin was lightly tanned, and she looked the picture of health. How ironic was that. And who would ever think that their child's weight loss was an indication that she was becoming addicted to drugs, that they were snorting the dregs of the earth up their noses, or shooting it into their veins, down their throats on a scarily regular basis.

I was horrified by the long-term use of the drug, which could apparently precipitate liver malfunction, permanent tooth darkening (of a greenish tinge), susceptibility to ulcers, and diminished sex drive. Then that word again – psychosis (mental derangement) – and how it can result in a 'hypomanic state': extreme mania.

Reading about the repercussions sent chills down my spine.

Some reports stated that CAT addicts suffer permanent brain damage and exhibit symptoms similar to Parkinson's disease. G-d, how could she even think of using this *dreckerai* (rubbish). The list of horror went on: death, heart failure, lethal overdoses, drug-related violence (which we are always reading about in the newspapers). My once protected world was spinning out of control.

I even became familiar with some terms used in the drug world. A 'line' is where the CAT, cocaine or heroin is shaped into a straight line either on a mirror or on any smooth surface where it is sniffed up into the mucous membranes of the nose and respiratory system. Wonderful.

Drug dealers, pushers, crack cocaine, ecstasy (methylene-dioxymethamphetamine) and the dangers of it, smack, china white, ludes, mandies, the pink lady (Wellconal). Then there was denial, repression, depression, projection, intervention, using, clean, tough love, NA, AA – it went on and on. Words. Words I had never heard of and had never expected would find their way into my little world.

I felt like I was a walking drug encyclopedia. But most of all I felt horrified, frightened and angry. What had happened to the beautiful baby girl we brought home from the Marymount in April 1975? What had happened between 1975 and now, to have turned her into a helpless junkie, an addict, spending her days lying, stealing, resorting to virtually anything to secure her next fix, ruining her relationships, hurting her family, losing her job... destroying herself?

How could she have put her life in such danger? G-d forbid it would be fatal. It could still be. And what if she was still using? Of course she was, a voice inside told me. But surely it was over? She had promised. I wanted to believe it so badly, but what if it wasn't? How many people stop, only to relapse after a year, two, five and more?

And the more I read the more addictive it became. It was as though somehow, with all this information, I would find the answer. A magic cure. So I continued to search for more information on the stimulation of heart rate and respiration, the feelings of euphoria, the loss of appetite, increased alertness, dilated pupils and elevated body temperature. I discovered that acute intoxication at higher doses may result in insomnia, tremors and muscle twitching, fever, headaches, convulsions, irregular heart rate, anxiety, restlessness, paranoia, hallucinations and delusions. The words bounced round and round my brain.

Every article I read had the same warnings, the same information. And it was all bad news.

Shite!

I wanted to wring her fucking neck. To bring all this onto herself and onto the family, such self-harm, such careless destruction. If I couldn't sleep before, when I didn't know, I really couldn't sleep with all the information I was now armed with. It had become all too clear, too scary. Addicts died from their addictions, they overdosed, they sometimes didn't mean to, they just did, it happened. It was all becoming too much. And throughout it all, I still had to contend with the creditors, the problems with keeping it all from Ma, the lies I got involved myself in, trying to protect her.

In all my reading I also came to understand that addiction is a disease, and you just can't wring someone's neck if they have a disease. You would not scream and shout at someone who had cancer, Parkinson's, or MS, would you? This was the greatest obstacle that faced me, getting my head around the fact that she had a disease. A *disease*.

Slowly I began to put the pieces together and learned that she had been 'using' for about 10 years. It started long before she met the hairdresser, so I certainly can't say it was his fault, but after she moved in with him, it got a lot worse. I learned how they had often holed up for the weekend snorting and sniffing away, dead to the world.

When I would invite them over for Friday-night supper, she would regularly tell me she was working late, or that she was nauseous, or had a headache. When I think of him sitting at my Friday-night table, both of them together, giggling, probably high as kites, I want to throw up. And I had no idea. Was I such a fool? Was I really that naïve?

I had believed that drug addicts were lowlifes from impoverished or broken homes, street people, holing up in public toilets, shooting themselves up. My mind went back to the movie *Requiem for a Dream* – how the addict ended up losing his arm because it had developed gangrene, and his mother had been hooked on her prescription tablets. Everyone seemed to be on some wild trip, and some girl was prostituting herself with some vile character to get her fix. People were desperate, shaking, out of control, hungry for their drugs. It was such a terrible movie, and that is how I imagined drug addicts: street people, sitting in gutters, desperate for their fix, desperate for whatever it was the drugs did for them, or to them.

I never thought of drugs addicts as just 'ordinary people', or as people from good homes like ours, with loving parents. I never thought of drug addicts as loving children, who adored their siblings, their parents, who were good at sport, and popular, leading ordinary lives.

I had never thought of drug addicts as being my own precious daughter...

Then I thought about those movie star addicts. Didn't Elizabeth Taylor drink herself into a stupor, spending time over the years in fancy rehabilitation centres? And Liza Minnelli, Judy Garland, Marilyn Monroe? What about them? They were all beautiful and talented. They were movie stars – surely they didn't have low self-esteem?

And what about all the singers and pop stars who had died from drug overdoses; cool, talented people, musicians whose music I had grown up with and loved? Back in the late 1960s – the time of psychedelic acid-rock, and Woodstock, hippies, flower children, flower power – Janis Joplin was all the rage. She was the 'Queen of Psychedelic Soul', a highly talented dancer, painter, singer and composer. She was inducted into the rock-'n-roll Hall of Fame in the mid-nineties. She was also an alcoholic and heroin addict and died of an overdose in 1970 at the age of 27 – found dead on the floor of her hotel room. Jimi Hendrix, one of the greatest guitarists in the history of rock music, died of a barbiturate overdose in London on 18 September the same year, also at the age of 27. A few months later, on 3 July 1971, Jim Morrison died of a heroin overdose in Paris, France. Elvis Presley, the King of rock-'n-roll, aged 42, in Memphis, Tennessee – the list is endless, the famous and the unknown, people tripping out on cocaine, pills, alcohol, morphine, Valium, cyanide, heroin, paracetemol, tranquilisers, opiates, painkillers, laudanum, Xanax. Famous people overdosing on drugs I'd never even heard of: fentanyl, chloralhydrate, temazepam, oxycodone, benzodiazepine, propanolol, clonazepam, bromide, secobarbital, ketamine, amobarbital, hemlock, mephedrone, alprazolam, lexapro, zoloft, veronal and speedballs. The stars we loved and revered under the influence of these toxic substances hanged themselves, slit their wrists, put a bullet in their brain, poisoned by the mercury content, overdosed both intentionally and accidentally on tranquilisers, cocaine, opiates, sleeping pills, and whatever else they could get their hands on.

Today it seems that half of Tinseltown is on drugs, and abusing alcohol. Look at Drew Barrymore, the gorgeous child star from *ET*, who was in and out of rehab as a teenager... Lindsay Lohan, a promising and brilliant young actress, getting herself arrested for drinking and driving every five minutes, violating her probation, doing jail time, and yet she's released – and no sooner is she out, then she's caught driving 'under the influence' again.

Mischa Barton arrested for marijuana possession, David Hasselhoff squirming around in his own vomit, Robert Downey Jr the jailbird, Nicole Richie the convicted felon, Macaulay Culkin arrested for possession, Charlie Sheen, Kirsten Dunst and Justin Bieber – and all those who succumbed to their addiction at the height of their success. Even today, news media is filled with the tragic stories of Corey Haim, River Phoenix, Heath Ledger, Whitney Houston, Amy Winehouse and Brittany Murphy. Philip Seymour Hoffman had been clean for 23 years before he relapsed and was found dead with a heroin needle in his arm. Stone dead. Terrifying.

As horrific and heartbreaking as these sordid tales of self-destruction were, maybe knowing that all these famous, glamorous people had the same disease as my daughter, in some kind of misguided way, made me feel better. Angela was the same as Nicole and Britney. Whoop whoop.

Anne as a bridesmaid at her Auntie Sybil Marcus's wedding, aged 7, Dublin Ireland, 1956.

Angela and Anne on Angela's first birthday party, 11 April 1976.

Angela, reading her favourite book from the Mr Men series, 1978.

Angela, Gregory and Anne, Eastgate, 1979. This photo was taken as a gift for Hymie's birthday.

Angela and Gregory, in the garden of their Morningside townhouse, 1981.

Angela in her King David Sandton Primary school uniform, 1983.

Angela in her Batmitzvah dress, September 1987.

Angela's beloved dog, Joey Dachshund, 2004.

Angela and Anne, on the day of Anne's nephew Mark Lapedus's wedding, 2002.

Angela and her Gran.

Anne and her partner, Lionel.

Gregory, Hymie and Angela, 2012.

Gregory, Gran and Angela on Gran's 90th birthday, December 2010.

Samantha Brest, Angela's sister, aged 19,
one week before she left this earth, 2004.

Angela, 2008, in the "Succah", a temporary hut constructed in the garden, with no roof, just palm leaves that we eat in for eight days during the festival of Sukkot.

Angela and her partner Stephanie, 2012.

CHAPTER 11

The blame game

Before the drugs, Angela had always been a very grounded child, a strong child, with a strict moral code. She was wise beyond her years, and she could always be relied on and be counted on. She was a wonderful sister to Gregory, she adored her sisters, both the older girls and the little ones, Samantha and Tiffany.

I know how much she hated it when I bitched about the 'maintenance' coming in late. And I hated myself for going on about it, but I couldn't stop myself. She'd hear me on the phone, rattling on and on about it, and really, at the end of the day, did it really matter if the maintenance was a week late? But I always had a fit about it. It was 1981, and I was working for a photographer. I worked until 2pm every day, so I could be free for the children in the afternoons. There were always lift clubs, school, netball matches, cricket games, chess tournaments and Ma would always help out. I would try to hold out as long as I could but if the maintenance hadn't come in by the fifth or sixth of the month, I would call Hymie, moaning.

'How the bloody hell do you expect me to manage if you don't have the maintenance here on time?'

Both the children had always felt the tension. They would hear me arguing on the phone with Hymie, terrible arguments that always seemed to end with me losing control and screaming, slamming the phone down, and then ranting and raving around the house. It must have been unbearable for the children.

After I found out about the drugs, I felt I was bordering on lunacy, chasing my own tail, living in a madhouse, not knowing what was happening to my beautiful daughter, not knowing if I really was 'enabling', not knowing if I was doing the wrong things, or the right things. And what were the 'right things'? All I knew was that my daughter, for whatever the reasons, was a drug addict and drug addicts often died from overdosing.

I have a friend from years ago – let's call her Margo – who confided in me that she suspected her son was 'using'. She said he was behaving oddly, that he worked hard, had a brilliant job, but had no money, was always borrowing from her and her husband, that he sold his guitar, and later his car, claiming he didn't need a car because he was on a fitness programme and preferred to cycle to work in Sandton City, about four kilometres from where they lived. I remember thinking it very odd that he would sell his car – the guitar, okay, I can understand that, but the car? Most young men his age, and he was about 26 at the time, love having a car. It's all very well wanting to cycle to work, but what about when he wants to take a girl out? No girl in her right mind is going to sit on the crossbar at 11pm at night coming home from a movie in Sandton City.

As a photographer who shot many corporate events, I had heard a number of guests speakers talking on addiction, on drugs, how they had managed to pull themselves out of the big black hole, saved at the eleventh hour from the brink of disaster, the claws of death. As a result, when Margo shared with me the signs her son was showing, I became suspicious. I told her that I thought he might be using drugs, and suggested that she speak to him, or take him for a drug test.

I remember Margo shaking her head in disbelief, despite her suspicions. He's just not that kind of boy, she'd said. He was a good boy, kind and gentle, very artistic, and if nothing else, he had his head screwed on right. He might be a little way out at times, but he was a considerate son, a reliable employee, and a doting grandson, and she was sure she was just being neurotic.

Thinking back now, she reminds me of myself: the denial, the disbelief. I remember wanting to shake her. Why was it so obvious to me, but not to her? She promised she'd talk it over with her husband and she'd let me know what course of action, if any, they would take.

'Ja, Annie, life's not easy, hey? Always something.'

Exactly seven months after our conversation, Margo's son was found dead from a drug overdose. He had been using for just over two years, and ended up in rehab to clean up his act. He had been doing brilliantly, and had not 'used' for three months. He then moved on to a halfway house but one weekend he got hold of his drug of choice, and ODed. The story goes that it was a 'bad mix' – and it killed him. He didn't stand a chance. He left his grieving parents, three sisters, an older brother from his dad's previous marriage, and a heart-broken *bobba and zaida*.

Margo's story terrified me. What if the same happened to Angela? I don't think anyone understands the dread and fear a parent of an addict goes through on a daily basis, watching one's precious child systematically destroy themselves and yet unable to do a damn thing about it. Maybe that's why it's easier to believe the lies – the truth is just too brutal.

One Saturday evening in 2010 Lionel and I arrived home around 11pm after seeing a movie in Hyde Park and Angela was on her way out. Before I could even ask, she hurriedly explained that she was on her way to the ATM at the Caltex Garage.

'You're drawing money at this time of the night?' I asked as I climbed out of Lionel's car. She had a strange look on her face, like nothing was going to stop her from going to draw the money.

'Yes, Mommy, I want to pay Helen tomorrow and thought I'd draw now so I can pay her early,' she said, cool as a cucumber, airy fairy, like drawing money in the dead of night was an everyday occurrence, and why was I making a big deal of it.

'It's not safe, Ang. The ATMs are deserted now. I'll give you the money for Helen, and you can draw tomorrow, or whenever, and pay me back. Besides, Helen won't mind because she'll have her money.'

I walked over to her and remember wondering at the 'look' about her – it's hard to define, even now – something in her eyes, the eyes that refused to meet mine. I didn't notice the size of her pupils (like they'd later tell us at the support group), because it was night-time and I wouldn't have known what to look for in those days. But that night she had a desperate air about her; she was in a hurry, she was talking very quickly and she seemed agitated, and now that I think back, I should have just told her there and then that she couldn't take my car. I could have stopped her. I should have. I could have taken my car keys from her, but I didn't. Maybe this is what people mean when they say I was 'enabling'? After all, wasn't that my car she was getting into? But still, somehow, I couldn't stop her. She wasn't a child, she was an adult. She was 35.

'I'm going. See you just now...' she said, jauntily climbing into my car (hers was out of petrol – again), and driving off.

'Why didn't you stop her?' Lionel asked. I was asking myself the same question. I could have easily done it, but something stopped me.

What was it that kept stopping me from saying *no* to her? Perhaps the fear that if I push her too hard she would run back into the waiting arms of the drugs, start the dance of destruction again, never come back, leave us forever. So I kept quiet, and just let her take the car, but inside I was seething. I bitched about it to Lionel as we walked up to the house, through the front door, all the way up the stairs, and right through the TV programme he was trying to watch. I couldn't fall asleep until I heard her key in the door hours later. She didn't pay Helen the money that she was in such a rush to go and draw, although she did give it to her a few days later. So where had she gone in such a hurry? Where indeed? Was this one of the 'disappearances' ex-Fiancée had spoken about?

CHAPTER 12

Blood test

When, in mid-2010, I suspected that Angela might be using again, the only house rule I made – at the suggestion of her counsellor, and to which Angela agreed – was that, at any whim of mine and without any reason given, be it in the middle of the night, or three in the morning, should I want Angela to have a blood test, I could take her to the clinic without any opposition whatsoever from her. We agreed firmly on that. And that is how I came to suggest a blood test the next evening, when I collected her from her evening with Ma. We had reached the top of Grayston Drive and I was already indicating to turn left into Rivonia Road to go drive her straight there.

She refused outright.

'Don't you trust me, Mommy?' she spat. She looked hurt, shocked by my outrageous suggestion; I immediately felt guilty.

Here she was, working her way through difficult times and I wasn't able to trust her. Mistrust had settled in after that first relapse when I found little plastic packets in her car a few months after she started her Twelve-Step programme, and I had run off to First Step with them in my bag.

Although she said they were old packets and swore she had not used and I believed her, I was only to find out much later that she had indeed used. She had relapsed.

So here we were, a year down the line, and I was still struggling to be firm with her. To say no. To be honest. Why was I always trying to stay on the right side of her? I needed to find the courage to say: 'No, I don't trust you, Ang.' But I didn't. So maybe I was an enabler after all – that stinging accusation I continued to deny so vehemently. The truth was that if this was 'enabling', then I was one big cowardly enabler.

'It's not that I don't trust you, Ang,' I lied, 'but we have an agreement, and you promised.'

But she wouldn't hear of it; she was adamant I was wrong, so I had to turn the car around in Rivonia Road and I drive us home.

We didn't talk. I was angry and she was sulking.

I heard her go out very early the next morning. She had no car so I knew that wherever she went, she was walking. Turns out she went to the clinic, had a blood test, and came home to proudly show me the receipt. It was obviously a tactic to make me feel guilty. She knew just how to get to me.

'See?'

I turned around from my work at the computer and looked at the receipt... but no, actually, I didn't 'see'. I didn't see why she made such a fuss, why she wouldn't go last night and why I hadn't just driven her there, finished and *klaar*. Why I hadn't just kept driving. What could she have done about it? But I couldn't do it. And even if I had driven her to the clinic, I couldn't have forced her into the doctors' rooms. And also, I hate to admit, but a part of me wanted to believe her, to trust her. I just couldn't put her through the indignity of it all.

Angela seemed awfully smug. She said she'd show me the laboratory's pathology report once she got it and flounced out of the room in all her glory.

Believing everything to be on track – of course that's what I desperately wanted to believe – I decided to do what I had been wanting to do for a long while: travel to Ireland, land of my birth, the land where I had lived until the age of almost 15 until we came to sunny South Africa, my parents, my brother Robert and I. To the land of sunshine and golden opportunities. They say you can take the Irish out of Ireland, but you can't take Ireland out of the Irish, and that is how it is with me. I love Ireland, or the 'oul' sod' as we Irish call it.

It was July 2010. The hype of the Soccer World Cup was riding high in South Africa, and Angela – filled with a sense of patriotism – went off to watch the opening ceremony at the Fan Park. Just before I left on my holiday, I took my cameras and a few other valuables to my brother and sister-in-law's home. Why? Well, of course it was just in case, but I suppose deep down I still didn't trust my daughter. I didn't trust her with my cameras; I was afraid she'd sell them. There, I've said it. I haven't been able to say it before, but I was afraid. I also wanted to get away from all the madness, and write a book about Ireland that I had started a year ago, in peace and solitude. Do something for myself after all the months of having to deal with Angela's problems, and escape the drama of everyday life with her.

I wanted to drive in the Dublin mountains, and revisit the places of my childhood, places where Robert and I swam, and walked, and played. Places where I had cycled as a child, with my close friends, and my cousins, many of whom were still in Ireland. I couldn't wait.

Lionel had pretty much recovered from his heart surgery, back to his old self, and I needed to get away from the tension at home, and just be 'normal' for a few weeks.

'Darling, just go, I'll take care of everything. I'll see to the doggies and you just relax over there.' Lionel was so good that way. He just wanted me to get away from it all and I couldn't wait either.

Angela presented me with the pathology report of her blood test the day before I left for Ireland. I took a quick glance at the document, but it was a typical computer-generated lab report and from what I could see everything listed showed 'Result: negative'. She was smiling from ear to ear, so why wasn't I? I threw the pathology report into my suitcase and, once I got to Ireland and away from all the madness, I looked at it a second time.

The names of all the substances for which she had been tested were listed: alcohol, amphetamine, barbiturates, benzodiazepines, cannabinoids, cocaine (metabolite), codeine, cyclizine, dihydrocodeine, EDDP, methadone, 6-monoacetyl morphine, opiates and phencyclidine. But, hey, why was the word methcathinone (CAT) not on the list? Why had she not been tested for CAT?

I called her from Dublin and I asked why CAT wasn't listed, and she explained that it was; that all the substances listed were the components that make up methcathinone (CAT). Sounded like a reasonable explanation to me... And what could I do about it anyway on the other side of the world?

So why, then, did I have an uneasy feeling in the pit of my stomach? Why were my antennae up? From thousands of miles away, I had a sense that something was not quite right, but I had no idea what it was. Maybe I was just being paranoid. Surely the test couldn't lie? At this point I was constantly on high alert, always looking for something, but I was never exactly sure what I was looking for. Was it just me being neurotic, fixated? The nagging feeling persisted but I shoved it away as best I could while I enjoyed Ireland, my Ireland, my homeland, where my dearest memories were still very much alive.

I arrived back in South Africa at the beginning of August. The second day I was back, I had a photo shoot, and when I opened my camera bag, the bits of broken lens hood – which I had replaced after an accident – were back on the camera, stuck on with duct tape for heaven's sake!

What on earth...?

Where was the new one?

Why was the broken one back on the camera?

Hadn't I thrown it out?

But there it was, staring me in the face. How could that be? I started to feel madness swell in my head. I immediately asked Angela if she could throw some light on the subject. She was clearly annoyed.

'Why is it that when something goes wrong, it's always *me*?' she asked defiantly. 'I haven't touched your camera, and if you remember correctly, you took it to your brother's house before you went to Ireland!' Her eyes flashed angrily at me.

She was right, I had taken my camera bags to my Robert's house, so how the hell did this happen? Unless she had switched the contents, of course... perhaps after I collected the bags from my brother's? Or before?

There I was again: questions, questions and more questions, my head spinning, and reaching the obvious conclusion that she must have done the swop before I took the camera bags to Robert. But what was the point? Why would she do that? Why? *Why?* What would be the reason for her swopping the lens hood? It seemed such a futile thing to do, and if there was a reason, what was it? But whatever it was, I couldn't afford – literally and figuratively – to have her fiddling around with my camera equipment. The lens hood had only cost me R500 a couple of months previously, and now it was gone. A whole other mystery surrounding a bloody lens hood. I felt like a woman possessed, making a fuss of a R500 lens hood when people are dying of cancer, hijackings are taking place, women and children are being brutally raped, animals are being tortured – and here I was going berserk over a lens hood. But it was the mystery surrounding it that was what was driving me mad, more than the actual fact that it was missing, that inexplicably my old broken lens hood was back in my camera bag.

I rang Sponsor, the one who had been helping her through her drug issues over the past few months. But instead of showing concern about what I had to report, Sponsor let me have it – from a dizzy height.

'You know, Mrs Brest, you are the very *last* person Angela should be living with right now, hey. In fact' – cough-cough, she went on – 'I'm thinking of having her moved out, and into a halfway house. Angela is my star sponsee,' she rasped on in her throaty, smoky voice, 'and the last thing she needs is this negative and distrustful attitude of yours.'

Huh? What the hell had Angela been telling her sponsor?

'Forget about all the drama you are so consumed by! Angela is doing very nicely,' she continued through her wheezing. 'She's entirely focused on her recovery, and I am not going to have you ruining that for her, hey?'

I felt like shite.

It felt like I was dancing a never-ending dance on shards of glass. Almost every day I would email my auntie Freda, call her on the phone, talk to Robert and Sharon, to Hymie, about my endless worries with Angela. Angela and I were also emailing one another because letters addressed to her were pouring in from creditors, most of whom were now threatening legal action. Over and over again, it was the same old story. All the signs were there... that things were not okay, that it was all heading towards catastrophe.

Then she had a car accident. She was not insured, and the car was a write-off. At the time, she lied and claimed she had been sober, but the truth was that she was so busy 'cutting lines' while driving that she never saw the Hilux one-tonne bakkie broken down on the highway right in front of her. She saw it a split second before ramming into it at 120 kilometres per hour. How she escaped relatively uninjured remains a mystery. The driver of the Hilux later stated that while they waited for help to come, he couldn't help but notice that she just sat on the bonnet of her smashed-up car, lighting up a cigarette as if writing off a car was a normal, everyday occurrence.

Of course she insisted it wasn't her fault, and naturally not a word was mentioned about the lines of CAT. She had been travelling at normal speed, she told us, and the truck had suddenly just appeared out of nowhere.

She had been on her way to a Brest family braai in Highlands North, Gregory was here on one of his yearly visits, and the entire family went to the scene of the accident to collect her for the braai. I had been photographing a corporate event, and it was Gregory who called me. I was devastated, but thanked G-d she was unharmed.

By October 2010, my inner bull terrier was on high alert. I suddenly got a bee in my bonnet that something may indeed have been wrong with that pathology report she had given me just before

I went to Ireland in July. So I rang the lab at the clinic to query it. Of course they wouldn't give me any information – I got this whole 'patient confidentiality' thing – and I just lost it with them. I ranted on and on about how nobody ever tells me anything, and that I had a lab report in my hand, that I was suspicious because my daughter went in for a blood test for CAT and while everything was ticked as 'negative' not once was CAT mentioned, by its slang term or its real name, or anything even close.

'What's your daughter's name?' someone with a clipped accent asked.

'Angela Shannon Brest.'

'When did she come in for the test?' Clipped Accent asked in between making me hold as other calls came through. Then I got cut off. I rang back and got through to someone else this time, but while I was busy retelling the story, Clipped Accent returned the call on my cell phone.

I gave her the details, the dates, Angela's identity number, and she promised they would get back to me. Finally, around lunchtime a call came from the pathology lab to say they had checked their records, but no blood test for CAT was done on Angela Shannon Brest.

'But,' she continued, 'Angela Shannon Brest did come in and have a blood test on that date in July.'

'So,' I asked, 'what test would that have been?'

I was told that she is not at liberty to disclose that. It was confidential information; that term again – 'patient confidentiality'.

Bugger that!

I got into my car, and drove to the clinic. I was there in under seven minutes, and marched into the laboratory rooms with her pathology report. I'm not sure what I was hoping to achieve, but I felt that same spinning feeling like I was on a carousel and couldn't get off. I was in a tailspin, and nobody was giving me answers.

I asked to see Clipped Accent but they told me that nobody from outside was allowed into the toxicology lab. I made a fuss, in tears of sheer frustration, and knew I was starting to raise my voice again. Then the timid receptionist, unnerved by what was about to unfold, quickly slipped into the laboratory, closed the door, and came out a few minutes later with Clipped Accent.

'Come this way, please,' Clipped Accent said, not looking in the slightest bit happy to see me.

I followed her into the toxicology lab and thrust the pathology report into her hand. She took one look at it, and excused herself 'for a moment' and when she returned explained that the report she was holding was a 'forgery'.

'What do you mean, a forgery?' I asked.

She explained that while the top part of the report was indeed Angela's ID, the date she came in for the blood test, and her contact details, the bottom part of the report that listed all the substances for which she was tested was not hers. She had somehow managed to combine the two separate reports and scanned them before presenting them to me. She also showed me a genuine report and it was immediately clear that Angela's was a fake. Hers was a dull green, the print not as sharp, whereas the original was a lighter green, the print pin sharp. She had forged the entire document, which of course is a serious offence.

I crumpled into a heap. My heart was pounding and I was shaking. Of course the only reason she would have done this was because she was not clean, and didn't dare take a 'real' test. Oh, she had been at the clinic all right – to take a simple blood test, one that anyone can take today and for which you don't need a script: a test for HIV/Aids. So that gave her the actual pathology report containing her ID, the date of her visit and all her data, contact details, and so on. That had all been genuine. Then she obviously got hold of another report – G-d knows whose, maybe someone she knew, another addict; maybe she swiped it from the laboratory at the time; maybe it was someone from First-Step who showed her their report and she copied it? No bloody idea, but it was manipulative, cunning, crafty and clever. But I had bust her – this time she had got a little too clever for her own good.

So the nightmare was ongoing. Why would she do that? Unless she was using again. Why forge a document? And did she not realise it's an offence to do so? She was lucky the laboratory didn't take the matter further. I think they just felt sorry for me, slouching there in a heap, clutching a pathology report in desperation. Desperate not only for answers, but desperate to know what was happening to my beautiful, grounded, practical, solid and stable daughter. I had wanted so badly to believe that she was all right, that my suspicions had been my own delusions. But now the proof screamed at me, unavoidable in black and white.

I phoned my brother and sister-in-law, I phoned Sponsor, I phoned her counsellor, I phoned First Step. I also phoned my friend Gaye Turiel who insisted I come over there and then. I was in bits. A total mess.

CHAPTER 13

Relapse repeat

I now felt that I was back to square one. On top of everything, our beloved dachshund Joey passed away four months after the fake pathology saga and we were all bereft. It was left to Angela to go to the vet to fetch his body, because I simply couldn't do it. In that way, Angela was very strong and always took charge when I was in an emotional state. I could always rely on her. She was like Ma in that way, always taking the initiative and getting things done.

Losing Joey was devastating to all of us. We couldn't deal with it. He had been part of our lives for 15 years of his precious little life. Losing him made me think of the day back in 1996 when Joey came into our lives. Angela was 21 and she visited the SPCA with a friend who was choosing a dog for himself. As they were leaving, she noticed a little dog who looked at her, and she at him – and from that moment on they were smitten with each other. She wanted to bring him home. I, however, wouldn't hear of it. '*Pleeeeeeeeeeease*, Mommy!'

'What kind of dog is it anyway,' I asked, one eye on my TV soapie.

'A dachshund, Mommy, and he's *sooo* cute.'

'A dachshund?' I switched off the TV. 'You mean a sausage dog? For G-d's sake, Ang, are you mad?'

'But, Mommy, he's so cute! Won't you just come and see him? He even has a name, it's Joey'.

'You have two chances, Ang! I have a million things on my mind, and the last thing I can think of, right now, is a *dog*... that's it, finished and *klaar.*'

Joey moved in two days later, lock stock and barrel, neutered, de-wormed, de-flead, and a shiny yellow leather collar around his scrawny little neck.

At the time I was convinced I had been mad to agree!

But the kids were smitten with him, and Helen fattened him up very quickly. It took a while, but I must say that the little fellow started to grow on me. I bought him his own bed, and bedding – a duvet and matching pillow – his own special dish, and his favourite food. As a result, he followed me around the house like a shadow. He had a way of looking at me, and I always had to laugh. He was a handsome little guy, too, eager to please, and just wanting to be loved.

We really loved Joey and losing him was like losing a family member. There were long Skype calls to Gregory in the States, me crying, all of us saying the same thing, over and over – that little Joey had had a good life, that he was a happy dog, that he was a loved dog, and that there was nothing we could have done to save him. We all said how happy we were that he died naturally, that it was just after a vet's consultation, and that we didn't have to 'do anything'.

About two days after Joey passed away, I found a small empty plastic bag and a tightly rolled foreign-currency banknote in Angela's room. It seemed to have fallen out of the pocket of one of her denim skirts, the fashionable one with ghastly tears across the thigh, the skirt she had worn two days ago when she brought little Joey back from the vet for his burial.

'But, Mommy, that must be an old packet... I haven't worn that for months now,' she said, laughing it off.

'Ang, you wore that skirt the day Joey died, I remember,' I said, this time courage kicking in at the absurdity of her deliberate lie.

'Nope, Mommy – wrong skirt,' she laughed triumphantly.

But I knew I was right. I knew it had been that skirt. I didn't say anything more to her right then, but I wasn't going to let it go. I know I always said that, but this time, I really meant it.

The very next day I phoned Sponsor about her 'star sponsee' and she immediately sent over a mutual friend to collect the empty plastic packet and rolled-up banknote. Mutual Friend and I sat on the couch together, I was heartbroken. Mutual Friend admitted that the packet looked like it could well have had a narcotic substance in it, but she would have to send it to be analysed before we could make any assumptions. I, of course, couldn't understand the significance of the rolled-up banknote, but apparently it's used for sniffing the substance up the nostrils. Mutual Friend also said she was pretty sure she knew where that foreign note had come from. Naturally, I asked questions, but she couldn't answer. Her loyalty was still with Angela; she was a good friend, of that there was no doubt.

That same week of little Joey's passing in February 2011 I was speaking to Gregory on Skype. It was not a happy call, both of us beyond upset at the loss of our beloved dog. But suddenly there was a fracas second to none… I couldn't quite make it out, but I heard Angela running up the stairs to the office with Chelsea (our pretty little female dachshund) and Lionel yelling his head off about *the dogs* (we still referred to Chelsea as 'the dogs' even though Joey was no longer with us) not being allowed upstairs. I remember him coming upstairs and Angela clutching the dog while Gregory, in America, still on Skype calling out, 'What's up, Mom?' Angela and Lionel were yelling at one another, and then there was a scream, a loud piercing scream, an unearthly screaming – it was me.

'Would you two *STOP!*' I was like a fishwife. '*Stop* it, *stop* it, *stop* it! I can't *stand* it. Shut up – both of you!'

I was screaming at them both. I didn't want to hear their different sides of the story. I just wanted them to *stop*. Gregory was calling out over the microphone on Skype, 'Hey, Mom? Mom? Are you there?'

'Would you all *stop it!* For the love of G-d – just fucking *SHUT UP!*'

My throated ached and my voice was hoarse from the shouting. I felt a sudden pounding in my temples, and I didn't care if I was making a show of myself. I felt like a 'fishwife', common and ugly, living in an ugly situation, my head splitting, angry with both of them.

Of course Angela should never have brought Chelsea upstairs. Doing so was like a red rag to a bull for Lionel. Personally I didn't mind if the dog came up, but Lionel had a thing about dogs not coming upstairs so I went along with it for 'peace and a quiet life'. But having said that, when Lionel saw Chelsea being brought upstairs by Angela in an act of sheer defiance – a kind of 'Fuck you, this is my dog and my house, and I will bring her up if I want to' – he should have kept quiet. But instead, he got high-handed.

He said she was swearing at him, she said he was the one swearing, but to be honest by that stage I was beyond caring about who said what to whom. I just wanted peace and quiet, I just wanted to talk to Gregory who was still waiting for me on Skype, and just I wanted to enjoy our *Shabbos* dinner. I just wanted to appear normal in front of Ma. I wanted my heart to stop pounding and I wanted everything back to normal.

The entire situation was farcical, so wrong, so bizarre. I was grieving the loss of our little Joey, and instead of us all being together as a family, here we were tearing into one another other. I returned to Greg on the computer, in an emotional heap,

'Mom? Hey, what's up?' He had been waiting.

'Greg, you don't want to know!' but I told him all the same. He was upset, worried, and felt helpless at being so far away. All Greg could say was, 'Leave it. It'll all blow over, Mom. It always does…'

But nothing was blowing over at all.

Angela moved that very night, before dinner. She had ran into Mutual Friend, who lived in Jukskei Park, and packed herself off to her place. That left Ma, Lionel and me spending Friday night alone, and Ma was devastated. What was going on, she wanted to know.

It may have been high time that Angela moved out anyway, but the circumstances under which she left had been dreadful. She had previously told me that she wanted to move out towards the end of February, because she had found a lovely apartment she would be sharing with a friend in Douglasdale. Another move. It must have been her seventh move in about 10 years. The Douglasdale friend was a recovering addict herself and she told Angela in no uncertain terms that she was welcome to move in, pay her share of the rent, but if she suspected that Angela was using, she'd be out. No questions asked. *Out.* Just like that.

For weeks Angela was angry with me, said I had sided with Lionel against her, and wouldn't come near me. She said she would come around when her anger passed. Lionel, of course, claimed I had sided with Angela and went into sulk mode. Oh, what a merry dance this was.

True to her word, when she left Mutual Friend's home, and settled down in Douglasdale, Angela started coming around again. Things were strained at first, but she thawed out after a week or two. Our Friday nights continued. Ma, Angela, Lionel and me. Awkward was not the word. Lionel and Angela ignored one another completely, and it was always so uncomfortable at the table. The Friday-night candles would be burning, but there was no peace at our table. Lionel sometimes went silent, and I tried to pretend I hadn't noticed, but at the same time, I also made sure I jabbered away to make everything seem normal.

Ma chatted away, too, and I was never sure if she was oblivious to the ugly atmosphere at our Friday-night table, or whether she was simply being diplomatic. Thank G-d for Ma... She chatted on and on about politics, about music, about her bridge, about everything, and to an onlooker it would have seemed just like a normal Friday night with a normal family sitting down to dinner in the glow of the *Shabbos* candles.

Nothing could have been further from the truth. This was *not* normal...

Halfway into 2011, in July, Lionel and I went to Israel for a holiday. When we came back, the first thing he did was to check his Kruger rands, which he had previously kept in a little red pouch in the office at home and then later in the *Pesach* cupboard in the studio. We felt they were safer there.

It should have come as no surprise to us that they were gone!

If I told him once, I told him a thousand times *not* to keep the Kruger rands at home, be it in the office or the studio. We then argued about that, me shouting about him having left the Kruger rands in the studio, and he shouting that that was not the issue; the issue was that Angela had taken them.

Of course there was no proof that she had taken them, and while I argued with him that maybe she hadn't, of course it crossed my mind that she may well have done. In fact, I was pretty sure she had. But, once again, as her mother I found myself defending her even though I felt I knew the truth.

Then started the big search dance for the Kruger rands. I searched the house, the office, the studio, my cupboards, my jackets, my handbags, my car, Lionel's car, I even asked my brother if I had brought them there for safekeeping when I had brought the cameras, but of course I hadn't. I checked the studio a second time, even a third, scouring every drawer over and over again. I looked behind books stacked in the bookcase until eventually I just couldn't look any more. The missing rands kept me awake at night and then I'd think of a place that they could be and I'd actually get out of bed and go look. But they weren't there. Of course they weren't there.

'Darling, please stop worrying about them. They're gone, don't worry any more,' Lionel said one night. I could see the pity in his eyes, and it upset me no end because I knew how devastated he was for my sake. But they were his Kruger rands and now they were gone. *Gone.*

And still I refused to accept that they had just *gone...* I was frantic. How could Angela have done this to Lionel? How would she ever have found them in the *Pesach* cupboard? Maybe we had moved them again? Maybe he had taken them to work? But he hadn't, and I knew it. It seemed that my life had become one big search... on and on, looking, looking, always searching for something to make some sense of this entirely absurd situation.

CHAPTER 14

Clean lies

Then, in the middle of all of this, just to add to the confusion, Angela announced she would be celebrating one year clean on 18 October 2011... Clean for a whole year? I immediately went into 'be happy, support your daughter' mode, and doubted everything I had been thinking about Angela and the missing Kruger rands, as well as everything else that seemed so out of kilter.

On Thursday, 20 October 2011 (coincidentally, Gregory's birthday), Angela was due to 'share' her story at a Narcotics Anonymous meeting at the church in Benmore to mark her one-year clean birthday. I desperately wanted to feel proud of my daughter, so I made sure I got there early. I arrived about 20 minutes before the meeting was about to start, and Angela and her friends were smoking outside in the gardens, with everyone making a fuss of her for achieving one year clean. Clean and Serene. Yet in my heart there was a dull sense of dread.

We sat around in a circle, and her dad and Felicité came too, with Tiffany, the youngest Brest sibling. When Angela stood up to make her speech, all my doubt dissipated and I was simply bursting with pride. How could I have distrusted her? This was a huge achievement; it couldn't have been easy for her to get to this point. I had listened to a few other people in the group share thoughts with the group, and it was obviously a huge struggle not only to get clean, but to *stay* clean. Everyone was congratulating her, so proud of her, so who was I to be suspicious?

Sponsor introduced her by saying a few lovely words. Her 'star sponsee' was clearly back on track, and I was so grateful to them both, to Sponsor for being there for Angela, and to Angela herself for reaching this extraordinary milestone in her life. She spoke well...

'Hello, everyone, my name is Angela, and I am an addict.'

'Angela!' everyone chorused in unison.

'If anyone had told me one year ago,' she continued, 'that I would be standing here this evening with one clean year behind me, I would not have believed them.' She thanked her sponsor and those who had been with her on her one-year journey, and spoke of how she alone was responsible for her own recovery, and how there was a time that she never admitted, even to herself, that she was a drug addict.

Angela spoke about honesty and being honest with others, but most importantly, be honest with yourself.

She spoke about how you have to hand over to a higher power.

She spoke about taking responsibility.

She spoke about determination and recovery.

And she spoke about taking it one day at a time.

I felt the relief wash over me, like rain after a devastating drought. The nightmare was ending. My daughter was finally on the right track, the right road. She had seen the light, and by the grace of G-d – and her own sheer determination – all the ugliness was well behind us now. I had heard her speak of 'getting honest', which meant no more lying and no more stealing. The Kruger rands were a distant memory – a terrible, terrible mistake. How could I ever have doubted her?

Angela had a friend in tow, a blonde woman of about 35, Blonde Girl, and she snuffled a lot of the time through the talk, tears welling up and very emotional. I'd never met her before and wondered who she was. I gathered that they weren't involved romantically; they didn't seem to be a couple at all, just good friends. She seemed very sweet, I thought, very supportive, and apparently very moved by Angela's speech. And I was happy and grateful that she was there for Angela. I was also happy that Hymie, Felicité and Tiffany were there for our girl, to share in her joy. As hard as the past few years had been for me, it had been hard for them too. She was our daughter, sister, friend, granddaughter, and she had scared us all shitless, but now – *Boruch Hashem* (Thank G-d) – it was all behind us.

Slowly, slowly. As Angela herself had said, 'One day at a time...'

For the first time in ages I felt relaxed. One year clean is no mean feat, and if she could do one year, she could do two, and three, and more, and then all this would one day become a distant memory. Way, way behind us. She was so determined to stay clean. I was proud of her.

Life was good after Angela shared her one-year milestone. She had a well-paying job, a nice car, her friends and a growing social circle. She was not involved, didn't want to get involved; she said she needed to keep all her energies focused on her recovery. She spoke a lot about her recovery and went to her NA meetings and did all the things she had to do for her own recovery. She knew nobody could do it for her. She seemed grounded again, and we spoke often, and Friday nights continued.

December 2011 came along, holiday season, year-end, when everything winds down in Joburg; people flock to Cape Town and to Umhlanga, or jet off to England, Europe, Australia, Thailand, and the United States. It's a time to relax and prepare for the coming New Year.

Lionel was so much stronger now, his bypass well behind us. I was supervising his diet, enjoying my photography assignments, remained fascinated by my genealogy projects, and had started to work again on my book about Ireland. Angela had been clean for over a year. And yet something was still niggling... In quiet moments, I couldn't shake this feeling of dread. It felt like my sixth sense was kicking in, telling me that something was wrong.

Of course, I couldn't quite put my finger on it, nor why I even thought it, but somehow I got a feeling that Angela was no longer at her job. There were no signs, no evidence; it was nothing she said or did, but the feeling gnawed away at me. So one morning, bright and early, I called her at the office, and she picked up the phone. Yay! So I was wrong. And so happy to have been wrong.

I knew I needed to back off, stop getting so edgy all the time. She had a good job, and was doing so well at it, so why was I getting my knickers in a knot every time I had a hunch for no rhyme or reason?

But, as it turned out, I was right. I didn't want to be right. I so badly wanted to be wrong. But during the course of the events that followed, I discovered that the day I had called she had answered by pure fluke. She just happened to be in the office clearing out her desk. I found out later that she was to be suspended from her job until after a hearing set for some time in January 2012.

Angela had relapsed. My first thought was, when did it happen? Was it after or before her 'one-year share'?

On hearing the sordid details, it was as though someone had stabbed me a thousand times. Apparently, the Douglasdale housemate had kicked her out when she found an empty CAT packet in Angela's room and realised she had been using. The Douglasdale friend had alerted Sponsor. Angela had then moved in with Blonde Girl.

I found this all out after a disturbing phone call just as we had sat down to supper in late January 2012. The call was from Sponsor...

'Mrs Brest?'

'Yes?' I answered cheerily, kind of happy in a way to be hearing from her. Maybe she has good news, maybe Angela is doing really well, and she's phoning to tell me.

'Please meet us all in an hour at a townhouse in Paulshof. I'll sms the address through to you. There is to be an intervention, and Angela will be there. It's not good. She doesn't know about the intervention yet, so meet us outside the complex please and we'll all walk in together and surprise her.'

I felt a rising panic, but at the same time some sense of relief, one sensation alternating with the other. Relief because it seems her friends had the same sense of uneasiness about her, panic because I had no idea what was ahead. I also felt pity for my lovely Angela and what was happening to her. Would our lives ever return to normal? And I felt anger – because it was enough already!

But my overriding thought was: What the hell has she done now?

CHAPTER 15

Intervention

Lionel drove me up to the townhouse, his lips pursed, his brow furrowed, an eerie calm descending over him, over us, as we made our way through the streets of Sandton. My hands were shaking, my heart thumping, my throat constricted, my trembling fingers picking at imaginary threads on the upholstered car seat. A sense of dread at every turn, at every traffic light, at the prospect of what was about to unfold. Finally – eventually – we pulled up outside the complex. Sponsor pulled up alongside us almost at the same time we arrived, and Angela's other friends were there within minutes of each other. Slowly we drove in convoy to the parking area. I felt guilty, disloyal, despicable, like we were ambushing her, all part of what seemed like some conspiracy.

Engines were turned off, and we talked in whispers; we need to catch Angela by surprise – and it was a surprise I knew she would not like. We all walked in together, nobody saying a word. Angela had just settled down on the couch. Was she surprised? I couldn't really tell. She had an almost Mona Lisa-type smile on her face, closed, unrevealing. She said nothing. My face felt tight, I wasn't smiling, I didn't hug her as I always do. I felt tense and uncomfortable. I felt mean and disloyal. I felt tired.

Sponsor sat down almost immediately. It was clear that this was not going to be a pleasant evening. Lionel said he'd wait in the car for however long it took, and Sponsor took the lead. Everyone took turns to speak to and about Angela.

I sat there opposite her, listening. I heard every harsh word, every gentle word, loving words; they all cared for her, that was evident from the start, but they had had enough. Enough of the lies, enough of the deceit. Most complained of having money, jewellery and personal items stolen. I heard about friends of friends who were all missing money, and while nobody had proof, it all pointed to Angela. It was unbelievable. How had my child become this thief? Angela sat, almost detached, listening and then denying, trying to keep her cool, but all the way I could sense that her denial was not strong enough, it was not going to see her through this ordeal. I kept thinking to myself that if someone ever accused me or even suspected me of stealing, I would have been up in arms. I would have laughed at the preposterousness of it all, or I would have become really angry.

But Angela did neither.

I almost wanted to call a halt to it all, to stop them from ganging up against my daughter, but the truth is that they were not ganging up against her at all. They were trying to help her. Although she was arrogant, she was also painfully vulnerable as she sat there on that couch, a lost soul. She had nothing but the friends in the room with her, but she couldn't see that they were on her side. That they were Team Angela. Most of these young women were recovering addicts themselves, and many had been in the same situation as Angela was in now.

Mutual Friend was one of those women confronting her now. She had always been a really good friend to Angela, but now she was emotional and angry. She had gone out on a limb for Angela, not once, but many times, and was this the payment she deserved? She spoke for quite a while. I remembered her sitting on the couch with me some months earlier when Sponsor had sent her to pick up the empty plastic packet and rolled-up banknote. Mutual Friend was fiercely loyal to Angela then and refused to speak out of turn, but now she said she had had enough. That Angela had betrayed her, let her down, destroyed her trust.

Then it was my turn. I thought I'd back down, or at least hesitate, my motherly instinct dictating that I protect and defend rather than attack and accuse. Instead, it was like the floodgates had opened. I had to grasp this opportunity with both hands, to take a stand, make my voice heard. So it was that I heard my quavering voice float over that room, heard myself complaining that she was giving me no joy in life, no *nachus* (the word I used automatically, and heard her translate to her friends as 'something like pride'). I admitted that I, too, had missed money and possessions over the last couple of years, and I never once got a satisfactory explanation. I heard my voice droning on and on. Sometimes gentle and hesitant, other times firm and resounding. I heard myself saying that if Blonde Girl kicked her out (as she was saying she would do by the end of that evening), I didn't want her to come home. I'd been there, done that, and I refused to do it again.

Was I really saying that? Did I mean it? I think I meant it when I said it. It sounded like the right thing to say. I didn't want to let her think that I was her port in a storm.

But a mother is a mother no matter what, and it's all about unconditional loving. And I knew in my heart that even if she didn't own up, if she didn't confess, didn't 'come clean', she would still be coming home with me. I would never let her be on the street – even though 'tough love' talks about that, tells you how this mother and that mother took a tough stance, and would not allow their son or daughter into the house, unless... But I was not made of that kind of tough-love material. I could not have done it. I would never ever want that. Was I a hypocrite, saying I wouldn't have her back in the house that night, knowing full well that if push came to shove there was no question about it? She would come home – rightly or wrongly. I could never take tough love to that extreme, even though I know it would have been the right thing to do and in her own best interests. She had to reach 'rock bottom', I knew that, but leaving her with nowhere to go is something I could not ever consider doing. It was simply not an option.

Blonde Girl was insisting that Angela had taken R100 out of

her purse, and that there was also her R40 000 diamond ring that had 'gone missing'. Although a couple of her ex-girlfriends still had a key to her place, which clearly meant that it was possible that any one of the girls could have been the culprit, she was intent on blaming Angela. She said that as much as it galled her, she would overlook it all, but there would be conditions. Angela needed to take responsibility for the ring, own up to taking it, and tell her where the ring was. That sounded fair to me and I agreed wholeheartedly.

The general train of thought that night at the intervention was that each and every woman there would give Angela love and support, but she had to be honest, and had to admit she was *using* again. It seemed she had recently failed a test, but now she had to own up to having taken all the missing things before her friends would offer her their support.

But Angela didn't own up, nor would she admit to using or stealing, and eventually they all decided to wash their hands of her. I was devastated. For Ma, for Greg, Hymie, all her sisters, but most of all for her. Where was her life going? What was her destiny? Sitting here, facing up against all her friends, would she end up with no one on her team? Yes, if she failed to own up, she would have to continue her journey of self-destruction on her own. They were emphatic about that. There would be no alternative.

Sponsor finally called for a tea break and she and Angela stepped aside for a little chat, and when Angela came back into the room she admitted to having stolen Blonde Girl's R100, that she had simply opened her purse and took it. But she refused to admit having taken the diamond ring. She insisted it hadn't been her. I couldn't help but think how anyone could keep a R40 000 ring in her bedroom anyway, but that, of course, was not the point... The point was that the ring was missing. And all eyes were on Angela.

I piped up, 'Are you short of money, Ang?'

'No, Mommy,' she answered, looking me square in the eye, like I had asked her if she was wanted a glass of milk or something. But I forged ahead...

'Well, Ang, then why did you take R100 from the purse?'

'I can't answer that,' she said more to herself than to anyone in the room, but still holding my stare.

I'm not sure if I was the one who said it, or whether Sponsor said it first, but suddenly the general consensus was now that the main problem seemed to be kleptomania rather than the drug issue. In retrospect, it all seems so unbelievable but there were indeed mumblings in the room that this could well be the case. While everyone was talking, Angela remained silent. I was sitting opposite her, looking at her, but now she refused to meet my gaze. I felt sick. I knew Lionel was outside in the car waiting – G-d, we'd been in the room for ages. Any other fellow would have been fed up, but not Lionel.

Sponsor called for another break. Some of the group badly needed a cigarette so we all traipsed outside. Angela went with Sponsor to another part of the garden, while the others all puffed away, everyone talking at once.

Although it was summer, there was a chill in the air. I was cold. I could hear a dog barking somewhere, and I remember shivering. Someone brought me a blanket and a cup of rooibos tea. What was taking Sponsor and Angela so long? I was tired. I was dying to go home. I had so much work to do... and clients would be coming the next day to collect their DVDs.

'Mrs Brest, would you like some more rooibos?' Some young woman with a smoker's cough was already taking my mug and heading to the kitchen to refill it.

They were good girls, all of them, all worried about and showing such concern for Angela, and I was the one who felt sick inside. Where was this all leading? If Angela had taken the ring, why didn't she just say so and face the consequences? But she swore blind she never did. Did I believe her? To be honest, I don't know what I believed. If she could take R100 then she could take anything, I suppose; but if she *had* taken the ring, then – as Sponsor had pointed out – she would have been out of her head, drugged up, smashed. A R40 000 ring would buy a lot of CAT. But she had not been *that* 'out of it'. So where was the money she would have received had she stolen and pawned the ring? There was no evidence of it at all. She would have paid off some of her debts, wouldn't she? That's a lot of dosh. She would have been dead on R40 000 worth of CAT.

'Isn't Angela a bit old to be involved in drugs? I thought that was for teenagers?'

Someone laughed. I suppose I sounded like a total fool.

'Mrs Brest, I only got my life together when I was well over 40,' someone explained.

'I had had one relapse after another.' I think it was Sponsor who said that. Sponsor was a very caring woman; she had had faith in Angela all along. She had always been there for her, no matter what, even defending her when I'm sure she knew or suspected that Angela had broken my camera lens hood a year or so previously.

Then Sponsor called us back into the room to tell us that Angela had something to share. We all trooped back into the lounge again. Angela sat down...

'I used,' she admitted, 'but only once – and I never took the ring.'

Someone commented that Angela had minimised her addiction by saying 'I only used once' and then everyone began talking at once, discussing what the next step should be. They were all hoping that Angela would admit to taking the ring, but she was still adamant that she hadn't. Blonde Girl was relentless in pursuing that line of thought, that Angela had taken the ring, and that was that. It seemed to me that the others were no longer as convinced that Angela had indeed taken it, particularly as it was now out in the open that a couple of other people had had a key as well... Now there was 'reasonable doubt'.

Thank goodness the lovely Collette stepped up. 'Angela can come home with me for a few days,' she said, walking protectively over to Angela. But Angela had to agree to get some help and admit to having used, albeit 'just the once'. The ring issue was no longer discussed.

Then suddenly Sponsor announced that Angela could spend the weekend with her at her place outside Johannesburg, away from it all, and they would have a quiet weekend, talking and trying to work out how they would proceed from here. She suggested that they could go through Step 4 of the programme: writing about all the wrongs she had done and all the people she had hurt. I couldn't help think that Angela might need more than a weekend.

But I was also relieved that people, friends, were offering to help.

CHAPTER 16

Rock bottom

In every book on addiction I have ever read, at every meeting I have ever attended, they refer to something called 'rock bottom'. Angela's Rock Bottom presented itself out of the blue on Friday, 10 February 2012 – after the intervention – and although I say 'out of the blue', of course it wasn't. It had been coming for a long time, brewing over the years, but when it finally happened, I guess it caught me completely off guard. Looking back on everything, how it had not happened a lot earlier beats me.

I was editing photos on my computer, waiting for my clients to collect their photo-shoot DVD when I heard the doorbell ring, followed by a rumpus, and I remember thinking how loud whoever was making that noise was. Like a flock of magpies, shouting and more shouting, and then Helen calling to me from the bottom of the stairs.

'You must come.'

'Helen, just send them up to the office.'

'No, no, you must come,' she called up, more insistent this time.

I popped my head out of the upstairs window, and saw who I thought were my clients, and Angela was there at the gate too. It seemed as though she was ripping into my clients, and they were shouting right back at her. I was mortified.

But then as I looked closer I realised it was not my clients at all.

They were strangers. Something was wrong. Helen was shouting, 'You must come! Hurry,' so I ran downstairs. Helen was beside herself, and there was Angela walking away from the gate with a strange man. And then I saw them. Handcuffs. She was handcuffed, and was being ushered towards an unmarked car.

The man accompanying her turned out to be a detective-constable from the Morningside Police Station, right next door to where we lived. A female officer stood next to him as he manoeuvred my handcuffed and near-hysterical daughter into the car.

What on *earth* was happening? I tried to stop him, ask the detective what was going on. But I couldn't make out what he was saying, something about her owing money. I heard some mad amount – thousands, I think, but I wasn't taking it in. I heard myself say I would pay whatever it was that had to be paid, but please not to arrest her. I would sort it out; just let her out of the car, I begged.

Out of the chaos I managed to make out that Angela had, according to them, tried to resist arrest, and the detective wasn't budging on taking her down to the station. Something about a R40 000 diamond ring. That's all I could fathom. That ring again! She was being arrested, being taken into custody, and because it was Friday, she would not get a court date until Monday. I felt the hysteria rising, my head spinning off my shoulders. Like something out of a movie, Angela was calling from the car, her head turned to look at me as she was whisked off, shouting out of the window: 'Mommy, come to the police station! Hurry!'

The police car sped off like a bat out of hell, and I remember thinking that he was breaking the speed limit of our townhouse complex and that Mr Brooks, our chairman, would go mad... But I grabbed the keys and my bag and Helen and I tore after the police vehicle.

By the time I managed to track Angela down in the labyrinth that was the police station, she in a highly agitated state, throwing her legs onto the side of the desk and slouching back in the chair. Between the lieutenant and the Detective-Constable M, and Angela chipping in every now and again, I gathered that Blonde Girl had laid a charge against her for the theft of the ring. I heard how the police had gone to the house in Douglasdale and she had refused to open the door. Something then about the Douglasdale girl's dog and Angela threatening to set the mutt on the police! She claimed she had been nervous, had come out of the shower to find the police in her lounge. They said she *knew* they were coming in, that the security guard had told her so. It sounded like a circus. I couldn't take it all in. But the bottom line was that Detective-Constable M was taking her to the cells, come hell or high water, despite her resistance. It was not her choice to make.

The rest of the day whirled by like a nightmare. Angela's life had spun completely out of control, disintegrating around her, and it had finally come to this. Now those tentacles of destruction had reached out into my own life and the lives of all the immediate family. We were all part if it now. Drugs had done that; they were like the large curling tentacles of a huge, greedy octopus, wrapping themselves around the family structure, strangling the life out of it.

Oh G-d, I thought of the neighbours who had driven past while the police were handcuffing her and carting her away. Had they seen the handcuffs? What would they be thinking?

With shaking hands, I phoned my brother and sister-in-law. They were distraught. And what were we going to tell Ma that night at *Shabbos dinner*? Where would I say Angela was? Even though Da had drummed into us from an early age that we should never use illness as an excuse – it was like tempting fate, he said – I decided I would just say she wasn't well, or something. Now, though, was not the time or place to think that far ahead. At some point in the middle of all of this I rang Hymie, and within minutes Felicité rang me back. When I got home, she and her younger daughter Tiffany were waiting for me at the house. Felicité was amazing. They both were. Despite a mile-long waiting list at Houghton House rehab, Tiffany had managed to secure her a place. I was so grateful. I was crying and bewildered.

What the hell was I going to do now?

At 2pm, I returned to the prison to visit Angela. The guards showed me into a small room and motioned me to sit on a stone slab that faced a crisscross iron grid. Through the grid I could see nothing more than a similar crisscross grid about 30 centimetres away. And then I saw her. She was on the other side, and in a reasonably good mood too – and that pissed me off big time. I mean, here I was, in a total state, and she was joking with one of the guards, the big deal that she was, cocky and full of lip. I was really angry. I remember that the room was noisy, and it was hard to hear her. She said she was hungry and told me she needed cigarettes, toiletries and a change of underwear.

I told her that Daddy and Felicité had come to the house.

'Is this what it takes to get Da to come to the party?' she asked cheekily.

But it wasn't a party at all. Angela would have to spend the weekend in the holdings cells. I was almost glad… At least now my worst nightmare had come to be. It couldn't get any worse. This was it. The living hell would come to an end. Something would have to change…

But when I got home, it did indeed get worse. Angela had left her filthy, pigsty car at my place, and I went through it with a fine-tooth comb. I carried everything into the house: books, files, packets, notepaper, empty cigarette boxes, matchboxes, DVDs, polystyrene cartons with bits of food left in them, whatever I could find. Amongst the garbage I found a slip from a pawn shop, then another. Four in total. What the hell, I recognised some of the items listed. '1 x 9ct pendant with coin.' But surely that was mine? Both Ma and I have pendants of King George and Queen Victoria. And '1 x 18ct diamond ring' (could that have been Blonde Girl's missing ring?), as well as a gold chain. There was a phone number on the receipt, so I called and spoke to a guy with some kind of accent. Yes, he knew 'Angellah'. She had been to his shop, he had the stuff. I must bring the money, he said, and I'll get it all back.

I went back to the prison around 5pm, taking Angela some cold roast chicken and a few rolls, a bottle of water, a few items of clothing (which the guards took to her cell for me) and spoke to her once again through that iron grid in the visitors' room, the horrible room that stank of stale cigarette smoke and other foul smells that not even the cloying smell of Jeyes Fluid could disguise. Alongside us, another couple argued loudly. Angela kept up some garbled story of which I could make no sense. She said the police had it all wrong, she had done nothing, and it was all some huge misunderstanding. The usual. Everyone else's fault but hers.

'Who's Yossi?' I asked her through the dirty iron grid, hoping she'd be able to explain the pawn shop. 'I found a slip with his name on it in your car.'

'No, Mommy, he's just a friend,' she chirped, confident as ever.

'Such a friend, Angela! He has a gold-coin pendant, a 9-carat gold ring, and a diamond ring. Is this by any chance Blonde Girl's ring?'

Silence.

'Answer me, for fuck's sakes, Angela.'

She didn't. I struggled not to raise my voice, even though I could feel a scream starting up somewhere near the back of my throat. I was determined to hang in. I told her with a calmness that betrayed my fury that she might as well tell me, because come Monday, I would be at the pawn shop first thing in the morning.

'It's granny's pendant... Greg's ring, and your engagement ring,' her voice was barely audible.

'Jesus!'

'I'm sorry, Mommy.' She was crying now, the first time I had seen her cry in years. But almost immediately she seemed to brush it off.

'Mommy, just stop worrying. I'll have the money... I'll get it all out for you again, I promise,' she gushed almost cheerfully. And for a second I believed her. I actually believed her. Again. For a split second, I believed she had the money and she was going to pay to get our stuff out of hock. Was I really doing this dance of sheer lunacy again? Believing yet another lie?

No, not this time.

'And don't forget to bring my cigarettes,' she called after me as I was leaving.

What is it about being a mother, that in the end, nothing matters but one's child? Despite everything that was happening, all I really

125

wanted was for her to be well. Sick as I was over the pawning of our stuff, it paled into insignificance compared to my need to have my Angela back again. Of course I was confused and sad, angry too – I have to admit that – but for the first time I realised that my child was sick. For the first time that addiction is a disease really made sense to me. She was ill. She had assured me that she had the money, that she would get the stuff out, but I wasn't waiting for that… I was going on Monday to do it myself.

Hymie got a lawyer, a smart Greek guy who knew his way around the prison protocols, knew the officers, knew the drill, and he tried everything he could to get Angela out on bail that weekend. But she hadn't been charged yet, so we couldn't post bail.

It was a Friday night, and all I could do was go to Robert and Sharon for supper. I tried to appear normal (Gaye Turiel would have called this enabling). Robert and Sharon knew, but not Ma. I told Ma that Angela was not feeling great and wouldn't be coming to supper. She looked so disappointed. Was I imagining it, or could she tell I was lying? I felt sick to my stomach. And what would we tell her tomorrow, and the next day? And the day after that? I was watching her watching her little great-grandchildren, and *kleibing nachus* (taking pride) from the whole scene. I was happy for her that she got such joy from my brother and Sharon's lovely family, but inside my heart was breaking.

Ma enjoyed it when my brother recited *Kiddush,* the Friday-night blessing over the wine, and how the children know it by heart – they were little more than toddlers – and then the ritual of washing our hands to the recital of the *Hamotzei,* the blessing of the *Challah* (*Shabbos* bread): '*Baruch Atah Hashem Elokeinu Melech Ha-olam Hamotzei lechem Min ha-aretz*' (Blessed be Hashem, king of the Universe…)

I knew I would have to tell Ma something. But what? There was nothing for it but to come right out and tell her. I couldn't sleep the entire night, my head was going over and over the conversation I was going to have with her. I tried to work out a plan of action, what I was going to say, and in my sleepless state, my plan of action had many different scenarios. In the cold light of day, I was dreading it. I wish I never had to do this, but who else if not me?

So once again, the next day, I went over to Ma's house, sat her down and started with one or other of the preambles I had worked out during my sleepless night. And then, suddenly, decided to just come out with it. She had just made herself a cup of tea and was sitting in her sun room.

'Uh, Ma... Angela has a bit of a problem,' I told her, as I sat down on the chair next to her.

'How do you mean?' Ma asked, concern immediately all over her face. I hated myself for having to say what I was about to tell her.

'She has a problem with... uh... substance abuse.'

'What's that?' Ma asked, putting her cup of tea back onto its saucer.

Oy vey... Surely Ma knew what substance abuse meant? But she was looking at me expectantly, so I told her – everything. Well, almost everything... I left out the miserable, shameful detail of Angela ending up in the holding cell at the Morningside Police Station. This was decided on by Robert, Sharon and me. We just couldn't face her knowing. I had toyed with the idea of 'in for a penny, in for a pound' but Robert and Sharon said it would just be too much for her and they were right. The sordid details would have broken her.

Ma was absolutely devastated. She couldn't take it all in; she had a million questions. She wanted to know how I had found out, and I went on to tell her that Angela had run out of money, as is often the case when people abuse drugs and alcohol, and in order to keep her habit going she had to help herself to money that wasn't hers. And I had started to notice money missing and confronted her, and she had come clean and told me about her drug use. I thought that sounded so much better than telling her Angela had robbed us all blind in order to feed her habit.

I stayed with Ma for about two hours, and she asked question after question. I tried to answer most of them as honestly as I could, although I confess that I skirted around a few. I mean, what's the point in hurting her even further? Ma wanted to know how it started and when, and how I knew, and whether anyone else knew. So I told her as much as I could. I told her about First Step and how the real reason for her break-up with Fiancée was because of her using. I told her Angela was flat broke, and how Robert and Hymie had helped me support her the year she moved back home. I told her that Angela was powerless over her addiction and now she was only too happy to surrender and admit herself to Houghton House.

Ma was quiet for a while, but I knew she was mulling it all over in her head, trying to digest what had just been dumped on her. Then she wanted to know what had led up to her agreeing to go to Houghton House. I said that Hymie and I had realised the seriousness of the situation, and told her we wanted her to get help, and she had agreed.

I didn't tell her about Blonde Girl and the ring and the Morningside Police Station. I just couldn't.

Robert rang me as I was driving home.

'So? How did it go?'

'I told her everything, Rob, except about the cells. I couldn't do that.'

Next bombshell. Blonde Girl refused to drop the case. She insisted that Angela was the one who had stolen her R40 000 diamond ring. Whatever the truth may have been, I could now see that it was in fact a blessing that this had happened, and as much as it pained and grieved me to see my daughter sitting in a cell, I felt a certain sense of calm and relief because now I knew things would have to change.

Hymie immediately called a meeting between the lawyer, him, me and Blonde Girl, who brought Mutual Friend along. Mutual Friend was very grounded, and I always liked her. In fact, all Angela's friends – mostly recovering addicts – were lovely. We met the lawyer on the Sunday at a restaurant in Randburg. Blonde Girl arrived looking flushed and harassed, her too-short fringe sitting at least three centimetres above her eyebrows, which made her eyes look as if they were about to pop right out of her head. The bottom line, she said, was that she was not prepared to drop the case. Hymie, his lawyer and I found her controlling and high-handed, but we kept our cool. She had come with a long list of demands. She demanded that Angela be sent to rehab. She demanded that Hymie and I set boundaries to which Angela had to promise to adhere. She was livid and spoke through gritted teeth. It was so hard not to lose it with her, hard not to tell her to back the hell off, and to watch how she spoke to us – we were Angela's parents, not some riff-raff off the streets. Nor were we naughty schoolchildren to be reprimanded like that. But we recognised that we were the ones on the back foot, and we didn't want to rub her up the wrong way.

There was absolutely no solid evidence that Angela had stolen the ring. I know it *could* have been Angela, but it could just as easily not have been her. The bottom line was that Angela's place was not in prison but in rehab, to learn lessons, to learn how to deal with her addiction, to go to lectures, see psychologists and follow the programme to get well again. That would not happen in a prison cell.

Thankfully, Hymie, Felicité, Tiffany, Robert, Sharon and I were all on the same page about that: we all wanted Angela to go to rehab. It was the only way forward. We had decided over the weekend plan that the plan would be to send her to Houghton House on our own accord, and the last thing we needed was Blonde Girl shoving it down our throats, threatening us with it. That night with the lawyer, Blonde Girl was making it sound like her demand for us to send Angela to rehab was something we had never considered, that this was her idea; and she was now holding it over our heads.

We went around and around in circles. While I cannot say that I blame her for being furious about her missing ring – particularly as it was a family ring, and if anyone can appreciate the sentimentality of that, it's me – but she didn't handle the session well. She was constantly on the verge of losing her temper, her face red, her voice quivering.

Mutual Friend, on the other hand, made a lot of sense; she was rational, she had good advice, and she shared how she and Angela were really close once and how she had rescued Angela time and time again. She told us how things had gone missing, the same old, same old, and always when Angela was around. But by now she really was '*gatvol*'. She felt, as we did, that things were so out of control that something needed to be done on a positive note – yes, rehab, if that is what it would take. Angela's life was so toxic that rehab was her only hope.

And who could argue with that? In the end, huffing and puffing, and still in a foul mood, Blonde Girl agreed to drop the case as long as all her provisos were met to her satisfaction. She left the conversation warning that she would be checking on us.

CHAPTER 17

Randburg law

I waited with the lawyer at the Randburg court on Monday morning, 13 February 2012. I remember it well, the day before Valentine's Day. How ironic. Angela was somewhere inside, in the holding cells. Although it was probably only an hour or two, it seemed like hours, the waiting. The plan was that our lawyer was going to ask the magistrate to release Angela on the condition that she went into rehab at Houghton House. There and then. That same day.

Our lawyer spent time with the magistrate, and it was agreed that the case was to be thrown out. There was simply no evidence whatsoever that Angela had taken that ring, and on hearing that Angela was going straight from the court into rehab, he had her released immediately.

She came over to where I was waiting. Instead of showing at least a modicum of gratitude or remorse – as one would have expected from someone released from incarceration – Angela was stroppy, cheeky, a smart aleck, abrasive and downright rude. I felt I was in a bad dream. I was afraid she was going to bugger off into the crowd, like they do in the movies, so I held onto her. She almost had a fit, and pulled herself away. She was irritable, grumpy, distant and arrogant. There were no tears, not a hint of an apology. She insisted that I take her home to fetch her clothes, but I was afraid she'd jump out of the car at the first traffic light and make a run for it. Now that we'd come so far, I was not going to take any chances. She went mad, angry. I was neurotic, she said, and what did I think she would do if I merely dropped her off to collect her stuff? But there was no way. She could be as melodramatic as she wanted, I wasn't buying into it. All I wanted was to get her into rehab, the sooner the better.

Houghton House is in Ferndale, Randburg. I had first heard about it years previously, through my friend Gaye Turiel. She had been the social worker there since the mid-eighties when it was still in Houghton. It was where addicts – kids stoned out of their skulls, on every kind of drug you can think of – went to clean up their act, to be rehabilitated.

When Angela and I arrived, we were shown around. I was struck by how beautiful it was. Gorgeous gardens, exotic bougainvillea creeping up the wall as you drive in, a calm and restful environment. The fact that I knew Linky Levin, one of the social workers there, made the check-in so much easier. She welcomed us with open arms, hugged me, and I felt tears welling up. She was Mother Earth herself and I clung to her, not wanting to let go. I had been carrying so much for so long. I really needed that warm embrace. She said nothing, neither did I, yet in that silence much was said.

Angela almost brightened up. She was no longer in the foul mood she had been in earlier at the court. I think she was glad, in a way, to get the help she knew she so badly needed. She seemed to have finally resigned herself to this. Surrendered. Like she was waving the white flag. Her life had been reduced to nothing but a series of lies and deceit and consequences. She had distanced herself from the family, so that her world was now one of addicts and addiction, dealers, powders and pawn shops. I remember the words of my friend Carol Zimmerman a year or two earlier: 'Desperate people do desperate things.'

It seemed Angela had finally come to realise that she was not in control of her life, her self, her emotions. Her entire value system had come crashing down around her. She had thought nothing of helping herself to what did not belong to her. For me, it made no difference whether it was R100 or R10 000 – it was all the same. So many people describe how their lives 'spiralled out of control'. Angela's had done just that. It reminded me of when I was a child and Da spun my spinning top for me – it would spin around and around, not stopping until it finally spun itself out. And those little wind-up toys would whirl all over the place until, suddenly, they would crash into a wall or a table. And then the eerie silence.

After registration, I found out all I needed to know about the rules, the dos and the don'ts, visiting days and phone rules and, once she was settled, I left. As much as I dreaded the prospect, I knew I had to get to the pawn shop, so I drove myself down the chaos of Louis Botha Avenue, mad taxis honking their horns, drivers shouting out their window to the adjacent taxi, people hawking goods at every corner and at every stop.

As I slithered through the door from the Louis Botha Avenue entrance, I hoped I wouldn't bump into anyone I knew, that no one would recognise me. I felt like a character in a seedy movie. This was not me. But it was now. As quickly as I could, I fumbled in my bag and pulled out the receipt, presenting it to the guy behind the counter. A few plastic bags of jewellery were plonked down on the counter. Some of the pieces in the bag were not mine, but the Israeli insisted that Angela had brought it in – he remembered her, described her as a beautiful girl. Greg's *Bar Mitzvah* ring was not there, so I asked for it.

'*Whot you mean is not all there?*' the Israeli asked, his thick accent failing to disguise his arrogance.

'But my son's *Bar Mitzvah* ring – it's not here.'

'*Whot it's mean? You don't belieff me?*' He called a colleague to come and assure me that this was *it*.

'*Yossi!*' he yelled. '*Angellah? She bring in other ring?*'

The two then switched to Hebrew, shouting at the top of their voice from shop front to office.

I wanted the ring, Greg loved that ring, it was his, he wore it all the time. I remember the day I had given it to him, the week of his *Bar Mitzvah*. He wore it on his middle finger then – you can see it in all the photos we had taken. In that dirty, claustrophobic shop I found myself smiling, remembering Greg on that day, 17 November 1990. We were so proud of him; he did the *leining* (reading from the *Torah*) as well as his portion. I remembered his speech too. I wouldn't let him read it, made him speak from his heart, and he did. I can still hear him. Confident.

'Angela Brest is a beautiful girl, not only on the outside, but on the inside...' Angela was beaming, in a white lacy dress I had made for her. She was 16 years old and quite striking. Gregory was like a little prince that night. I was *kleibing nachus* from both my children – you can see it on the *Bar Mitzvah* video and in the photos. The *Bar Mitzvah* wasn't easy for the family; it never is when divorce means that there are two families to consider. And to make it worse, Bobba (Hymie's mom) had inadvertently been left out of the speech. But now, according to Jewish Law, Gregory was a 'man'. Thirteen years of age. He was ready to take his place as a member of the community, and make his family and their family before them proud. He was a little *mensch*.

'*Mah at ratzah memeni? Whot you want from me?*' the man called Yossi shouted, bringing me back to the here and now in the filthy pawn shop.

I could feel the tears. Yossi was ranting on about how I could buy another ring, and in fact, he had one just come in two weeks ago and maybe I would want to see it? Angela had sworn that the deadline to retrieve the ring before it was sold was not yet up, that there was at least a month's grace, but it was clear that they never had it. Obviously, the ring had long gone.

I slithered out of the shop again, dived into my car and drove home an emotional heap. It's not the jewellery, it wasn't even the money, it was the whole experience. The seediness, the desperation of it all, that I had to do this – go to a pawn shop to buy back some of my own belongings.

I was worn out, with no energy left to even be angry as I drove home. The same honking, the same taxis, but I didn't hear any of it. I got myself onto the highway and headed back to Morningside.

In the meantime, Blonde Girl was on my case. She was emailing me and texting me. Day in and day out. Cc-ing our lawyer and Hymie. Demanding her ring back. She was virtually accusing *me* of having that blessed ring. But I didn't have it. Had never even seen it. In fact, I didn't even know what it looked like. So I asked Blonde Girl to send me photos, and she sent me a drawing. I had definitely never seen anything remotely like it. It was a beautiful ring, four diamonds in an elegant, classic setting. I assured her, and reassured her that I did not have her ring. And still she wouldn't get off my case, hounded me, insisting that the ring was at my house. It was when she made veiled threats of sending the police to my home that I had had enough of the madness.

I went directly to the Morningside Police Station, and almost insisted that the detective-constable come to my house. I showed him the jewellery I had retrieved from the pawnshop and he agreed, loud and clear, that there was no sign of Blonde Girl's ring. Of course, Blonde Girl wasn't buying that. She was fixated and in the end I had to have our lawyer bat her off once and for all.

Back at home, I again went through all the items from the pawn shop. Some I didn't recognise at all – G-d alone knows where they came from – but one item was a little gold watch that had belonged to Lionel's daughter, Laureen Gilinsky. Lauren was only 24 years old when she had been tragically killed in a motor-car accident on her way to Swaziland with a friend. Lionel had got the call, the one every parent dreads, in the middle of the night. He had kept a few items belonging to her, items she'd had with her in the car, in a small jewellery box returned to him by the traffic police all those years ago.

I felt sick to my stomach that Angela had pawned that watch. It was worth nothing, maybe R100, if that, but it was one of the few possessions Lionel had of his beloved child. Angela herself could identify with that – she had lost a sister some years before, and she knew how death left the family bereft. Yet she chose instead to get her fix, to shove CAT up her nostrils. To get high.

We had lived through a turbulent few years, the constant lies, stealing and deception, and I always found myself wondering what it was about a drug called CAT that stole my Angela's dignity, her pride, her value system, her morals, her self-worth. Up until the time of CAT, Angela had never as much as touched my purse, let alone taken from it. She had very high morals; she was ethical, and honourable. To be reduced to what she had become, CAT must have such a strong hold over its victims that they think nothing of overstepping the boundaries of honesty. Of course, we all have choices, and Angela's choice could just as easily have been to not use CAT, or any drug. But she chose it, and now it had trashed her. Obliterated her morals and her beliefs.

Drugs, in whatever shape or form they come in, are like parasites clinging to their respective hosts, owning them, their thoughts, their lives and their very souls. Even when addicts tell themselves that they want to try to stop, the voice of the parasite is louder, imprisoning them in its web of addiction.

The whole drug scene – the users, the dealers, the pushers – is like a cancer. For every addict who is in remission, and fighting to stay clean, there are thousands more getting hooked by the minute.

And there is always someone willing to sell this poison to our children. The more I uncovered about the drug scene the more I became aware of how deeply entrenched the drug network is. Right from the top: from the drug lords and drug barons, the hugely wealthy kingpins or traffickers, right down to the dealers, and pushers who get their supply from the dealers and who then go out to peddle on the streets, these leeches live off our children, off somebody's husband, brother, sister, wife, daughter…

Our children caught up in the terrible web of addiction lie, steal and pawn our things to pay for the luxury homes, million-rand cars and extravagant lifestyles of these parasites. And there seems to be no end to it. For every drug bust, 10 more cells spring up. Why would they stop? They are hell bent, motivated by money. These dealers, pushers, traffickers have everything to gain financially, and conscience doesn't come into the equation – they care about nothing except the money and the power they have over the addicts, our sons and daughters.

As parents, we spend thousands – hundreds of thousands in

some cases – to send our children to treatment, to rehab, sometimes over and over again, in order to motivate our addicted loved ones to stop. But how do you motivate dealers and pushers, kingpins and barons to stop? And as long as there are people out there pushing drugs – from the ice-cream seller outside the school to the guy peddling drugs in the dark corner of a club or alley – there is a chance that our children will get hooked. From all the books I have read, all the meetings I have attended, it all starts with someone offering the addict that first taste – and there is always someone waiting in the wings to keep the addict in supply.

This is especially true when it comes to teenagers. Dealer leeches know how vulnerable and impressionable young people are; they know there's a need to fit in, to be 'cool' and 'popular'; they know all about peer pressure. No dealer ever cares that someone's life – the life of their entire family – is being ruined, as long as they are paid. As long as the money comes in.

I thought of my daughter's life, once so bright and promising, now so messed up, a tangle of fraud, theft, pawn shops, and finally prison and rehab. And all for what? To enrich some dealer who saw her as little more than a ticket to the good life, quick cash. It almost killed me to see that my daughter had been a pawn in this tragic game of drugs, that she had become just another statistic, just another addict whose life bore all the scars of a life ruined by drugs. I prayed that she would pull through, that somehow she would be able to pick up the pieces and rebuild a life.

CHAPTER 18

Moving forward

When I began writing this book, I made an appointment to meet with Alex Hamlyn, the co-owner/director of Houghton House and The Gap. Angela had now done four weeks at Houghton House and recently graduated from her four months at The Gap. She was living in a halfway house near Northcliff. I was shown into Alex's office. He shook my hand, motioned me towards an armchair and I sat down.

He was very direct, and explained what Houghton House was about and what their aims were, but as hard as I tried to concentrate, I struggled to take it all in. It was almost too much to absorb. Certain words did, however, get through to me, and while they scared me, they also reassured me.

Alex talked of primary care, secondary care, of interventions involving detoxing the patients, different therapies in which they attempted to dismantle the defence mechanisms that had been supporting the patient's addiction. I also understood that they had did group therapy, family therapy and written work. They were 'didactic', he said (at the time I didn't even know that didactic meant intending to teach). There were help groups where information was given by the therapist about the nature of addiction and the road to recovery. Alex spoke of diagnosis, illness, therapeutic approaches, and how patients were encouraged to accept that they had a problem with addiction. Words like 'responsibility', 'going forward', the Twelve-Step programme, Alcoholics Anonymous, Narcotics Anonymous, support, recovery.

He was direct, to the point, factual, knowledgeable, experienced, tall, immaculately dressed and downright bloody '*gorjus*'. As flippant as that may seem, it was a bonus in all the chaos and sadness – some eye candy that proved a welcome distraction from all the crying I was doing inside.

'In secondary care,' he explained, 'the emphasis shifts slightly away from dealing with the addictions directly and it encourages patients to explore other struggles in their lives, including trauma, and relationship difficulties.' I was transfixed. I listened to him talk about teaching life skills, communication skills, stress management and problem-solving, while at the same time looking at how these struggles can contribute to relapse potential.

There was more about group therapy and individual therapy and how they provided an environment of self-awareness and again that phrase about taking responsibility, as well as ongoing professional support – all vital when making any attempt at recovery.

I had been encouraged to join a support group in January 2010, at the same time that Angela had joined the Twelve-Step programme at First Step in Sandown. I was only too happy to go because I felt the need to be with people who were also experiencing drug addiction within their family unit. I needed to be able to relate to the stories of others. I desperately needed this. I was nervous, but also strangely excited. We were 15 people all together, 12 women and three men. We met every Monday evening at the home of the woman who still runs it – Barbara. She had a soft, gentle voice, and listened intently when we talked. I found great solace in that group, I still do. I needed to be there because when I talk to friends, as supportive as they are, it's not the same as talking to people in the same unfortunate boat – kindred spirits. I needed to be with people before the meeting started, to talk, to share things. We have eats and at the end of our time together we say the serenity prayer. Sometimes I feel so stupid saying it.

'G-d grant me the serenity to accept the things I cannot change, the courage to change the things I can, and the wisdom to know the difference…' And then we would say more, still holding hands, something about 'if you work it, it's worth it', but I could never get it right. I still can't. I just say 'it works – you're worth it, you're worth it, you're worth it.' Nobody noticed I had it wrong because they all look down and close their eyes, but I never close my eyes as I fumble through it. It doesn't mean anything to me; it should, but it doesn't.

Still, in one way, I always looked forward to the meetings, but also dreaded them at the same time. Everyone was so supportive; we all listened to each other's stories, some tragic, some less so, but somehow it helped knowing that we were all kindred spirits. We were all from different backgrounds, different religions, colours, races and creeds, but joined together by the very thread that brought us all to the group in the first place.

It was one of our Monday-night meetings. We all sat in a big circle.

'Maybe it was my fault?' I said, fishing in my bag for a peppermint.

'No, Anne, don't think like that. It's not you,' Barbara reassured me in her gentle, soothing voice. But I wasn't convinced. It had to have been me. Something I did or didn't do. I was the parent she lived with; I raised her. Maybe I was too strict? Or not strict enough? She had always felt that Gregory was the favourite. Could that have triggered her off, set her on that downhill journey of self-destruction, that spiralling out of control? Where she could put her hands into another woman's handbag and take from it, where she forged documents, and cooked her credit card statements to show that she was in the green. Did I do this to her? Could I have?

'Anne, are you listening to me?' Barbara was asking.

'Yes. Yes, I am,' I answered, embarrassed.

'Look at me, Anne,' she said, knowing I wasn't paying much attention.

'You see,' she continued, 'we don't know why people use drugs, we don't know why they start. Some try it and never continue, others try it once and are hooked. Some people have addictive personalities and before they know it they're hooked and can't stop.'

I was crying. I thought I had it bad – until Rayna told us that her 24-year-old daughter had been a heroin addict. Through hard work and sheer determination, she had managed to get off it, and after a celebratory family dinner to mark her 'one year clean', she had gone home and decided to give herself a shot. That night she jumped off the balcony of her fifth-floor apartment. Miraculously, she survived, but had broken her back and was now a quadriplegic writing her life story with a ghost writer she had met in rehab.

'Her whole life was ahead of her,' Rayna cried. 'Why did she do it? Why? She had struggled so much to get clean, worked at her sobriety. She did so well.'

The story sent terror through me. It could happen to any of our children.

'Maybe she wasn't ready for the big celebration. Maybe we shouldn't have had the dinner for her? She didn't really want it; she didn't want us to make a fuss, she said so, but I insisted on us all going out to celebrate.' Rayna was crying so much we could hardly make out what she was saying.

Everyone in the group had terrible issues. I didn't know whose was worse. Miriam had issues with her father, and cried during the sessions; it was gut-wrenching to see and hear her cry. Some of us simply looked down into our laps, not sure what to do, but Barbara would go over and wrap her arms around her, and say soothing words, and hold her, until the wracking sobs would subside.

Jenny, another young woman in her early twenties, with a three-year-old child and a brand new baby, had just found out that her husband had been using for years. She had never suspected a thing, until someone from his office told her. Jenny had refused to believe it, wouldn't have anything to do with the person again – until, a few months down the line, she started to notice that things were going missing at home. First the camera was missing, then the laptop was gone, then money, and more money.

'I'm... like... finished. This is *so* not happening!' Jenny cried, her face red with anger, furious with her husband, struggling to understand (as were all of us at the time) that addiction is a disease. She talked about leaving him, the sooner the better. What the hell! This was not for her, no way. But then… The tears flowed, and she admitted how much she loved him and wanted her marriage to work. Why did this happen? Was it her?

Listening to everyone share their stories forced me to look at Angela and our story and I was forced to ask: Why did it happen? Was there anything we could have done, should have noticed? Maybe there *were* signs, but I never noticed, didn't even know what to look for. No one in my circle of friends smoked dagga or used any kind of mind-altering substance, so how would I know?

I've never used anything in my life. Never touched a cigarette, no alcohol and certainly no drugs. Of course that doesn't mean I didn't know what dagga smells like. And I know what cocaine looks like – you certainly see enough of it in the movies, the fine, white powder all neatly pushed and shoved into a straight thin line and then snorted, whoosh, up one nostril, and then, whoosh, up the other. I've read about coke addicts whose nostrils eventually cave in, collapse because of the ravages of cocaine. I know, too, that heroin is usually injected into the veins.

As a youngster in my late teens and early twenties, lots of people I knew 'used'. A lot of the folk singers smoked dagga in popular clubs such as Nite-Beat in Hillbrow and the Troubadour in Joubert Park. So many songs were written under the influence of dagga, laughingly about fields full of beautiful, red flowers and strawberries as they passed a joint from one to the other.

That's what I noticed: people who smoked dagga seemed to laugh a lot, used a lot of slang, had a faraway look in their eyes, like they were seeing something we weren't. And they probably were. How many folk-singing parties and braais had my friend Linda B and I gone to, where everyone was smoking except us. Joints were passed around, there would be lots of alcohol available, and the room would be filled with cigarette smoke. Linda wouldn't touch it, and neither would I. Ma would have had a blue fit if she knew that we went to places where dagga was smoked. We enjoyed being part of the folk-singing group, we loved listening to people sitting cross-legged on the floor, eyes partially closed, as they sang, and laughed. And if ever there was peer pressure, it was then – everyone wanted Linda B and me to be part of their mind-altering experience, but we were adamant that we were not going to partake.

They also smoked at the Yeoville swimming pool and at socials in the Yeoville Recreation Centre. Folk would get all giggly and laugh a lot; they said how 'healthy' it was to smoke dope – 'Nothing wrong, my china' – purely 'recreational', they could stop at any time, at any give moment; it was just a 'gas' to smoke some now and then, and, besides, they saw things so much more clearly, became more creative. Whenever people smoked at parties, you could smell the sweet, cloying smell, and I would watch the smoke swirling around in the room, everyone laughing hysterically. I would feel like March Hare at the Mad Hatter's Tea Party, and I remember thinking how daft a scene it all was and how I never wanted to touch it. And never did.

Barbara did explain, however, that I was an 'enabler', that we all were. We were enabling our children, our loved ones, our spouses, in their respective journeys of self-destruction. I simply could not understand this at all. How could I be enabling my daughter to do the very thing I was devastated by? It made me appear as though I was giving her the money and telling her to go and buy the stuff and use. Enabling? *What the hell?* I was being made to feel that I was as good as supplying her, helping Angela get the drugs... I resented the implication, and resisted the concept completely.

I regard myself as a reasonably intelligent human being, but for some reason, I could not get my head around the fact that I was enabling my daughter. Barbara said I could call her at home if I was desperate. And sometimes I did.

All I know is that I was looking for answers, answers that were proving very hard to find.

Then I joined a co-dependency group, which Gaye Turiel ran from the *Chabad* in Riverclub. We were a small group of four. All lovely women, and I looked forward to the Tuesday meetings. Again the subject of 'enabling' came up. I was an 'enabler', I was told. Again. I began to hate the word, the entire premise. The hell I was! I could not and would not see it at the time.

I asked Gaye about 'enabling' because it was bugging me that I was being referred to in these terms, had been given this label – 'enabler' – as though I had some kind of a disease. Gaye slowly explained that it didn't mean I was helping her to 'use' drugs, but rather that I was helping her to preserve, protect and maintain her addiction, either by covering up for her or assuming responsibility for her behaviour, making excuses for her, denying her dependency, stifling my feelings, playing the role of martyr.

These things were hard to hear. I didn't want to see myself that way but I tried really hard to stay open-minded. I could see that I made excuses for her, I agree that perhaps I did assume too much responsibility for her behaviour, and I admit that I did pussy foot around her a lot. But it was only because I didn't want to push her away by being high-handed, I didn't want to pick her out about all the cigarette butts lying around the garden, or that filthy cap always plonked on top of her head for fear of pushing her back to drugs. I was always terrified she would start using again so I did everything in my power to be laid-back, kind and non-judgmental. I know I often chose not to see that she was lying, choosing rather to see only the good, the positive. But I knew, too, this attitude wasn't helping – it was the ostrich's head-in-the-sand syndrome. I could see that. Perhaps this was indeed 'enabling'.

On the advice of a few people, I also joined a 'tough love' group. But if I struggled with 'enabling', I was no good at all with 'tough love'. Before any of Angela's drug problems came out, I remember hearing Adele Searle give a talk on drug addiction years ago at a Liberty Life conference when I was the photographer, and I remember how she had said that there's a time when you just have to use tough love. She went on to explain her approach and her own experiences, but I knew I could never do it. You have to have nerves of steel, and I just didn't have what it takes to turn your back on your daughter – an extreme measure that tough love sometimes required. Even though I could see that it might have been the right thing to do, it just didn't feel right to me.

There were about 18 people in the Tough Love Group, including two frum Jewish women in *sheitals* (wigs) whose children I knew – and couldn't believe that they were drug addicts. Another couple I knew from *Shul*, all of us in the same drug-addict-children boat.

The stories were shocking. One couple spoke a lot about their troubled 16-year-old son, how he had struggled to get clean but couldn't stay clean. He had stolen their car one evening a few weeks earlier and had an accident in it, so now there was to be a court case. He tested positive for booze and drugs at the scene of the accident and they were worried that he would be sent to prison. He killed himself soon after his parents shared their story in the group, leaving his parents and two sisters bereft.

Another woman, Victoria, had a son of 27, a heroin addict who had managed to get himself onto the right path, he went back to university, got his degree and had a rosy future at some up-and-coming finance company – only to relapse after three clean months when he shot himself up with heroin. He ended up in a clinic and was found trying to jump out of a third-floor window, by a male nurse who had gone to the ward to check on him.

One bloke's wife had run off with the local butcher, leaving him with their three teenage sons, a seven-year-old daughter, and a sad, arthritic dog of almost 15. Over the last five years, his eldest son had graduated from dagga to a whole cocktail of drugs, and finally heroin. The man was a broken soul.

Every week the stories became worse than the week before. It was depressing, but in some ways, I would leave feeling better knowing that I wasn't the only one out there, that my issues with Angela paled into insignificance compared with some of the struggles of others. But it terrified me that it was perhaps just a matter of time before her problems, our problems got worse. Knowing that there are always people worse off than you or your loved ones doesn't change the facts. My daughter was a drug addict – difficult for me to say, but a fact none the less.

Many people, including myself, don't initially understand why or how others become addicted. It is often wrongly assumed that drug abusers lack moral principle or willpower and that they can stop using simply by choosing to change their behaviour patterns. But, in reality, I have come to understand that addiction is a complex disease, and giving up using takes more than good intention or a strong will. In fact, because drugs change the brain in ways that foster compulsive abuse, giving up is extremely difficult, even for those who are ready and willing.

There was so much evidence around me of addicts who were not able to stop, of addicts relapsing and even losing the battle with drugs that I wondered whether my daughter would ever be able to stop. But I knew I loved her and would never turn my back on her and that if ever she needed ongoing love and support it was now.

CHAPTER 19

Clean (for real)

I visited Angela at Houghton House once a week and brought her cigarettes, chocolates, biscuits, fruit and cold drinks, shampoo and other toiletries, whatever she needed. It was February 2012. Everything had to be checked in on my arrival so that nothing undesirable went through the gates.

She asked me if I had told Ma and how Ma had reacted. I told her that Ma was having a hard time with it, and just for now she was not yet ready to speak with her – but she would be very, very soon. She was hurting, but not angry. She just had to give Ma some time to get her head around it all.

A week after that, Ma arranged a time to phone Angela, and they spoke for the first time since Angela had been admitted. Neither ever told me what was said in that conversation – it was private – and I never asked, either Angela or Ma. But I was happy that they had spoken. I knew it meant everything in the world to Angela that Ma had wanted to make contact.

In the meantime, Angela was thriving and flourishing in rehab, and she seemed to enjoy my visits. We would sit out on the lawn, the residents with their families, on rugs, chatting, eating sandwiches and apples, chocolates, cold drinks all out on the blankets. Little children ran around, some swimming in the pool, and it all looked like one big family picnic.

But a picnic it wasn't. It was hard work for the residents, the recovering addicts. Their lives were a series of meetings and lectures, they had chores, they cooked, and through it all they struggled to control their longings and desires for their drug of choice. During her time at Houghton House, Angela was only allowed visitors on certain days, and at certain times, and I chose Sunday as my day to go, while Hymie went on Saturday afternoon.

After four weeks Angela was able to move out of her primary care in Ferndale and entered secondary care at an outpatients' facility known as The Gap next door. Her new privileges included more visits and I could also go during the week. She was doing well, she took her meetings very seriously, she visited children at the orphanage, and she cooked for the house when it was her turn to do kitchen duty. She worked hard at her recovery and also made many meaningful friends. Some had been with her at Houghton House, but a number were new friends. Friends who, like her, were learning the programme and learning to stay clean. I asked her if she would like to see her gran and immediately the tears welled up in those beautiful almond-shaped eyes of hers, and she nodded that she would. I asked Ma that evening if she'd like to accompany me on visits to The Gap and she was delighted.

So I started to take Ma on my visits. She was thrilled to see Angela, and Angela was equally happy to see her gran. Their bond remained unbroken despite everything. Nobody mentioned a word about anything other than what she did every day, what she was learning, her chores. We would sit in the winter sun chatting while people walked around, some enjoying visits from their families, others simply listening to music. Angela would introduce us to her housemates, her roommate.

What was most clear was that Angela was getting better. For one thing, she began to look entirely different, no longer dirty or unkempt, but clean, almost shiny-clean. (It's taken some time for me to learn that the word 'clean' has a whole new meaning when you are an addict.) Her skin was glowing, she was glowing, her hair shone – she wasn't wearing that filthy suede hat any more. She was no longer so aggressive – she was kind, caring, loving, and smiling. We were thrilled to see her like that, so happy to have our daughter back.

Every Wednesday, come hell or high water, I went to visit Angela at The Gap and continued to take Ma with me without fail. Ma was amazing; she never once admonished or questioned Angela (although I did have to sneak Angela her cigarettes while Ma wasn't looking). Our focus was now on Angela's recovery, and not on why she did what, or when. As a result, our times together were meaningful and special. Angela had gained quite a lot of weight during her stay, which we saw as a positive, because now that she wasn't using she was eating again. Oh, happy days.

And when we would leave Angela would always walk Ma to the car and hug her close. It was almost as though nothing had ever transpired over the last few years. And although I knew Ma struggled to fully grasp it all, she handled it well, quietly, diplomatically and with dignity. Always the lady.

The one thing Ma did struggle with, though, was that Angela had stolen from her. She took it so personally that Angela had taken her jewellery and her traveller's cheques, that Angela had had the gall to walk into her bedroom while she was preparing supper, and help herself to jewellery she well knew would be hers one day. I kept on trying to explain that it was not personal at all, that Angela loved her with every part of her being, and she would never ever have hurt her, but the lure of the drug was much stronger than morals, than rationale, than value systems. I tried to explain to Ma that drugs are like a cancer, eating away at their victims' code of ethics, lurking within, and owning their addict. I explained that Angela was now learning to have power over her addiction and not let it own her. It was hard for me to get this across to Ma because I was only barely starting to grasp it myself – the concept that addiction is a disease.

One *Shabbos* morning, just after the service, Ma – completely out of the blue (for me, that is, she had obviously been mulling over this for months) – asked whose decision it had been for Angela to go into rehab. I told her that Hymie and I had decided, which was true – well, we didn't have a choice. But then I wasn't going into the history behind our 'decision' with Ma, seeing as it was a family decision to spare her the straw that finally broke the camel's back: the prison cell. It would have killed her if she were to know that her 'beauty' had spent a weekend in the holding cells of the Morningside Police Station. But Ma had asked Angela the same question a week previously, and Angela had said it had been *her* decision and apparently Greg had said it had been *my* decision.

Ma is a very astute woman, and she must have sensed that we were keeping something from her. She kept telling me that whatever it is the family was withholding, she'd rather know than not know, which made perfect sense. I'm like that myself – I'd rather know and deal with the issue at hand – but still I couldn't tell her. As I write this, she still doesn't know and somewhere between the time of this story being finished, and the book being published, we know we have to tell her. Angela and I discuss it sometimes and neither of us is sure how we will do it. But we know we have to, withholding the truth is not an option.

Bright as she was, Ma wasn't buying my story. She told me that each one of us had given her different answers about how Angela had ended up in rehab. Ma always says that to be a good liar, one has to have a good memory! Apparently, the first time she asked me what had led to Angela being admitted into rehab, I had said that Angela had realised she needed help, that she could no longer cope on her own, and had decided to admit herself to Houghton House. I hated lying to Ma, and I had tripped myself up in the process, but there was no backtracking now. I felt like a rat in a corner and instead of trying to get out of it, instead of backtracking, I just didn't have the energy, so I lost my temper. Shame on me for that. Ma was 91 years old – where was my respect?

'Why can't you just bloody well leave it alone, Ma! Let's just move on and be happy that Angela is getting the help she so desperately needed and wanted!' Which, of course, made it worse. Ma was right of course, but her persistence in trying to drag it out of me was getting me down. That's not her fault, it's mine. My conscience for keeping something back. I was angry with Angela for getting us all into this situation, angry with her for ever starting to use in the first place. She was already an adult when she started to use, not some flighty, clubbing, freaked-out teenager out on a *jol*, determined to paint the town red.

Ma fell silent then. I had hurt her with my outburst, and I knew it, but instead of blaming me, I was blaming her.

Part of the Twelve Steps is about making amends to those you have hurt. And to my way of thinking, it was time now for Angela to make amends to the family. Certainly to my nephews, to Ma, to Hymie and Felicité, Tiffany, and myself, not to mention all the friends she stole from. We had all been part of this wild dance, and while she never took anything material from Robert and Sharon, she certainly stole their peace of mind, causing them untold anguish and pain. I wanted her to own that, to say sorry for my Ma's sake, for mine, and for Angela herself. But nothing was forthcoming.

Although Angela did go and see Ma, and make amends, she approached no one else with any word of remorse. I couldn't understand it. I had been asking her for a couple of years now to make amends to my nephews. My brother expected it, and from his (and my) perspective, that was the right thing to do. But she always said she wasn't 'ready', and she would do it when she was. Robert asked me over and over when Angela was planning on making amends to the boys, and I kept telling him she would do it after Step 8 or step-something-or-other. But he felt that she shouldn't need to work on some step to be able to say sorry to the boys and give back the money. It wasn't even that much money – it was more the principle, and I agreed with him. I took her to task about it, and she said – as she had said on previous occasions – that she would do her amends in her own time, when she was ready, and not before.

Angela has promised many times that one day all my questions will be answered. I still have the need to know what really happened to my iPod, my cell phone, a second cell phone, our missing US dollars, Lionel's Kruger rands. She never admitted to having taken the coins Lionel missed from his American coin collection – until I found them when packing up her Douglasdale apartment, along with a few insides of watches I had given Ma, brooches, tools, and a Middle Eastern letter opener that one of Lionel's boys had bought for him.

People do want some form of an apology. I know I do. It helps with closure, helps to alleviate the pain in some way. Perhaps it's no more than an acknowledgement of the suffering we have all been through. Maybe 'apology' is not even the correct term here, but some form of acknowledgment, some form of communication about what happened over the years. I have a need to have my own mind put at rest.

After five months at The Gap, Angela moved to a halfway house in Northcliff. Time went by. Angela collected her clean time, marked by little coloured keyrings from NA meetings. They were like badges of honour in the personal war against drugs.

Then, on 3 January 2013, Angela was one year clean – for real this time. She celebrated her clean birthday by sharing her story of hope and strength at one of the rehab centres, as well as at an NA meeting in Rosebank. I took my long-time friend Joel Kahan with me; he has always liked and cared about Angela. We all sat in a circle out in the garden, they said the serenity prayer and a few people shared their stories, and then Angela shared with the group how her life had been. She spoke about her lying, her cheating and her addiction. She was unflinchingly honest. I was so proud of her that night.

Angela moved into a new home in North Riding, a new beginning and a new phase in her life. There was a new straight-gone-gay girlfriend in her life, someone she had met in recovery, and although it is suggested that you don't get into a relationship in early recovery – because your focus needs to be on recovery, rather than the relationship – Angela had reached her landmark of one year clean and she and Stephanie were sharing a good and healthy relationship by this stage.

She also got a new sponsor, someone she'd been asking for for a long time and who suddenly became available for her. New Sponsor is fabulous. I met her parents once years ago, in Ireland of all places. I know how much New Sponsor means to Angela and this warms my heart.

In May 2013, a few months after her birthday share, my good friend Patti Geber was going to Australia and asked me if she could buy some Aussie dollars from me. I had brought some back with me and I was happy to oblige. But when I went to look for them, they were gone. G-d forgive me a million times, but my thoughts flew to Angela. Could she have taken them? I was struck by the memory of how back in 2008, when I came back from New Zealand with some US dollars, they had disappeared, never to be seen again. Oh, Sweet Jesus, not again... Surely not! But then where were they? And then the search-the-house dance started all over again. Could I have possibly cashed them in at the bank and not remembered? Did I perhaps spend them at the airport in Australia and not bring them back at all?

I found them a few days later when I picked up a book – they were tucked between the pages! Sorry, Angela... Sorry, sorry, *sorry*.

How long would this go on for, the suspicions, the angst each time I missed something? Would my suspicions always fall directly to Angela? Does that ever go away? And if it does, when? I felt so guilty for daring to think that Angela had stolen those dollars. She had been clean for over a year by then, she'd gone back to her Oral Hygiene profession, she shared a lovely home with her partner Stephanie, she was attending meetings regularly, and she certainly seemed to have got her life back together again.

But I also know that addiction can creep back at any time. There are many examples of people with many years of recovery behind them who have slipped... And I pray each day that my daughter is spared that.

CHAPTER 20

Unpacking the lessons

People often ask me how Angela is getting along. I proudly tell them how well she is doing, how well she looks, how happy she is, and I share with my close friends that my trust is now coming back. I no longer hide my purse, I no longer question her, I no longer read her mail – I no longer even have the desire to do so. Nobody calls the house looking for her. She is working her programme and managing her finances. I am thriving on the knowledge that she is well again, clean again, and moving forward.

But would I know if she wasn't okay?

The truth of the matter is that I probably wouldn't have a clue. All those years, I never knew. I didn't. Nothing looked different, she seemed the same as always. It was only the lying that eventually caught up with her – and even then it took me 10 years to notice! And I am not an unobservant person at all. But addicts are so clever, cunning; they are able to lie with a straight face, and remember their lies. Angela always remembered what she told me, and stuck to it, but if she ever contradicted herself, she was always quick to correct it – quick as a flash. She had a way of looking at me, so innocently, and I always believed that there was something the matter with *me* for doubting her. She had us all fooled, even her sponsor.

They tell us at the support group that we are not responsible for our children's addictions – we were not the cause of it, and we cannot fix it. But there was, and still is, a little voice in my head, a persistent little voice that is always wondering, playing the guilt card. Maybe it *was* me? Was I too anxious, too neurotic? Did I worry too much about money – or the lack of it? Did I destabilise her with my own little pity parties, my mood swings? Maybe I overdid it, maybe I should have been more in control of my own emotions and not lost it in front of the children. Was that part of it? Did that turn my daughter into an addict?

All the questions, all the guilt. But then I find myself pushing that little voice aside, and remind myself that I was – and am – a good mother. So maybe I made some mistakes along the way. Perfect, I'm not. Never was. Never will be.

I loved both my children with all my heart, and gave them everything I felt they needed – even if they didn't, like those clumsy-looking Doc Martens boots Angela once wanted and I hated. But I bought them anyway. I worked hard on giving my children a sense of worth, a sense of values. I taught them good manners and respect. There were always birthday parties, movies, outings, and sleepovers. I always hugged them and kissed them because I loved them so much. And they knew it.

My children grew up in the bosom of all my wonderful Sandton *Shul* friends, and their children, one huge big happy family. I did what moms do, lift schemes, judo lessons, tap-dancing, swimming lessons, watched their school sports, prize-giving, but most importantly I think I gave them all the love in the world.

And I think about all of this now simply because it is always difficult for a mother to fathom where they may have gone wrong. When I look at the situation rationally, however, I know it was nothing I said, or did, to make Angela use drugs. That was her choice, just as not using cannot be anyone else's but hers.

CHAPTER 21

Owning my disease

One of the most valuable things I have learned on this journey of healing with Angela is how powerless I am over her and how I have to step back and allow her to recover and not try to control the outcome of things. That is very hard for any parent to get right, especially when you see that your child is in crisis and needs to be rescued. There are days I get it right and there are many that I still it get terribly wrong.

In this time of Angela's recovery I have also begun to look within at my own addictive patterns and have come to some sobering realisations. Although I have never smoked, never had a drink, and never touched a drug, that doesn't mean that I have been spared an addictive personality.

You just have to watch me around a box of Ferrero Rocher to see just how addicted I am to chocolate, and I am definitely addicted to my computer, my cell phone, Facebook – and there have been times in my life where I have definitely been addicted to being 'in a relationship'.

Before I settled down and met Lionel, I couldn't function unless I had a boyfriend or 'partner'. Very often they were men I knew were no good for me, did not share my value system, had issues of their own, but I was desperate to be 'in a relationship'.

A number of years after my divorce, I met a man. He was

charming, crazy about me, full of compliments, and gave me endless attention. He whisked me off my feet; nothing was too much trouble for him where I was concerned. He was a Gregory Peck look-alike, tall, dark and madly handsome. He had a great sense of humour, great dress sense, was kind and generous, divorced two years, and had three little girls similar in age to Angela and Gregory.

It was a whirlwind time. He was a nice guy – and he was my Mr Nice Guy. He called me twice a day, wanted to be with me morning, noon and night, booked DVDs for us to watch together, invited me to weddings, braais, his company year-end party. I lapped up all the attention, and in time he started bringing his children over to play with my kids. He invited us to the country club to which he belonged, where he played golf, and while the kids played together I sat and chatted to the golfing wives. I loved that some of the women would knit or crochet and talk about book clubs and movies, dangle bits of gossip about who was doing what with whom. I felt like I fitted in and loved it all. The kids got on famously, and there were outings to Warmbaths (now Bela-Bela), to the Bunny Park, to birthday parties, swimming parties. I thought I'd died and gone to heaven.

But soon another side to him began to emerge. Mr Nice Guy would disappear into the shadows, and his alter ego would take over. He was moody and unpredictable. Very. Sometimes a whole day would go past and he wouldn't phone. I would sit and wait for the call, sometimes not moving from the phone in case he rang. If I rang him, he would be irritable – 'Just going into a meeting' and 'Can't talk'. My anxiety would start revving up. Was he going off me? Was there someone else? Had he changed his mind? I began to feel terribly threatened, and longed for his call, his embrace, his attention. Sometimes when the phone rang, I'd make a dash for it.

'Hello?'

But it wasn't him. I would be so mad I could spit, hating the caller because it wasn't him. Why wasn't it him? Where was he? From twice a day to this?

What's happening?

Then he'd call. And he would be in a great mood. He'd come over with his girls and take us all out for supper, Ma included. Nothing would be too much trouble. Sometimes I would suggest that the younger children share a meal otherwise it would be a waste.

'Doll, what are you worrying about? So the worst thing that can happen is that they won't eat it all!'

But just as I got used to Mr Nice Guy, the other side would emerge again. I began to notice his temper, which he didn't hesitate to lose at the slightest provocation. He didn't get on with one of his sisters – not that he treated his mother all that well either, and they say if you want to know how a man is going to treat you, look at how he treats his mother.

The more distant and aloof he became, the more obsessed with him I became. When he didn't ring me, I couldn't concentrate on anything. I became irritable at home, impatient with my kids. Whatever outfit I wore looked wrong, my hair was wrong. I longed to be with him every minute and hated the times apart, which were becoming more often. He was my drug. Yes, Mr Nice Guy was my drug of choice. When he was attentive and loving, and on our weekends out with the children, I loved my life and everything in it.

But after about a year's courtship, things really began to wane. I could feel it. He was a misery most of the time, spoiling many outings with his bad attitude. His eldest child had major problems and was in therapy, and one day she knocked over a vase in the sun room. Emily (Ma's domestic worker) saw her do it, but he wouldn't believe it. We argued. He was just so unpleasant and I started to wonder what on earth I was doing with him. I started my tug-o-war thinking. Dump him and be alone? No, no, no, not an option. Put up with him and be irritated? Yes, yes, yes. Better that way. I was like an addict bargaining with using and abstaining.

In my heart of hearts, my better self wanted it over. I was still young. I'd surely meet another man one day, so why did I need to put up with this? But I couldn't end it. I kept making excuses. He was nice to my children, generous with them, made them feel important, and this was surely worth a lot. On the other hand, this made his own children jealous and resentful, and it was only a matter of time before the children started arguing with each other.

Who needed this?

I took the problem to my cousin and best friend Brenda who had seen me in floods of tears for over a year and who only wanted me to be happy. She said, 'Anne, he's not consistent – what good is he if he showers you with attention one moment, and cold-shoulders you the next? You need this like a *loch in kop*. So be without him for a while, so the children won't have the outings to the Bunny Park. *Nu?'*

But then before I could do the chop, he dumped me first!

I was heartbroken, devastated, in bits, broken. What a catastrophe. I cried, begged, pleaded, implored him not to leave me'. Forgotten were all the things that made me decide to leave *him*, his selfishness, his mood swings, his temper. I couldn't eat, sleep or work. I became obsessed. I was on the phone to him morning, noon and night begging for another chance. I was needy and clingy. I lost three kilograms in nine days. I was a wreck. My friends couldn't understand me at all.

'But, Annie, you *wanted* out.'

Yes, yes, true, I had, I did. But now I didn't.

Eventually, after almost seven weeks, he decided to give it another go, came over with flowers and a speech, and said he loved me. He was going to work at making us work, he wanted me in his life, and we were going to be one big happy family. Sounded great to me. And I welcomed Mr Nice Guy back with open arms.

For a week I was in heaven, ecstatic, on a heady high. Life was worth living again. Yay! I was so happy to be a 'couple' again and have a 'family life' for the children. I sang around the house, and sang all the way out to the car, all the way to work. Life was great, amazing, fabulous, I was so *happy*.

But once I settled down to being back in the relationship again, all the reasons I had wanted to end it came pouring back, and I would wonder what I was doing with him. I wanted out.

He irritated me, didn't appreciate me, stopped seeing me as often as I would like him to. He had annoying habits – he was an annoying *person*. He didn't get on with his brother and sister-in-

162

law. He was pedantic, petty, obsessed with politics and cars. He just wasn't a nice person. I had to end it.

But I could never just 'end it' there and then. I'd always have to wait for the right time. Bargaining. Delay tactics: 'I'll end it after his birthday, after my birthday, after *Pesach*, after the July holidays, and then after *Rosh Hashanah*, after year-end.'

And then, before I knew it, a year had gone by and it was another one of his birthdays coming up and then it would be my next birthday and I still hadn't dumped him. I'd moan and groan to my friends about him, how it was 'enough already'. But then why was I still in this relationship? Why did I want to be in a relationship with someone I didn't really like any more? Some of my friends said they'd rather stay at home with a good book than go out with a man who got on their nerves.

But I could never end it, so when he dumped me a second time, claiming that I was too needy, too cloying, and always in his space, once again I was devastated, panicky, broken, rejected, wounded, hurt, insecure and I begged, once again, for him to take me back! I was forced to ask myself why I had wanted to spend time with a bloke who got on my nerves. I just so loved the feeling of 'belonging' and I loved the 'family feeling' when he'd come over and take us all out, his kids, my kids, and me; it was the 'togetherness' that I loved and needed. But it was all a fantasy, really – an idea, not the reality.

After listening to one of my crying fits over the phone, Brenda instructed me to meet her for coffee where she gave me a book called *Obsessive Love* by Dr Susan Forward and Craig Buck. *When it hurts too much to let go* was the subtitle.

I had read *Men Who Hate Women and the Women Who Love Them* by the same author and Robin Norwood's *Women Who Love Too Much*. The very first thing that hit me as I started to read was that so many people in both books were 'Anne'. Different names, different cases and different circumstances of course, but we all had one thing in common: a neediness, like a hole in the soul, an emptiness that drove us to make unhealthy choices.

I read many case histories, theories, about women from

alcoholic homes marrying alcoholics, and men with controlling mothers marrying women just like them. Stories of misogynistic men, and women who were controlled by them. Men who were real charmers at first, but who turned into nightmarish monsters once they were married.

I saw myself in so much of both books, and if I read and understood correctly, it would seem that my needing a man in my life stems from my childhood. Da was a really good man, but life had dealt him a terrible blow in 1952 and he simply couldn't cope. He was frustrated, and often in an angry rage with life and everyone in it. He didn't provide for us – he couldn't – despite loving us. The memory of his sad hugs are with me still.

It was Pop and Granma who paid for my music lessons, elocution for Robert and me, our clothes for Jewish holidays, and outings to the seaside every Sunday in summer, and Ma, in her quiet way, kept the house running along on as well-oiled wheels as she could.

The books brought up many uncried tears in me. Was my search for love in serial relationships not to do with me looking for something to fill the missing space of Da? Was this not a life story repeating itself? It had just never occurred to me before. Angela and I had both experienced – albeit for different reasons – no father active in our day-to-day lives. Ma played the same role in Angela's life as Granma played in mine. I saw clearly how in many ways Angela and I were the same; she simply looked for solace in drugs while I looked for mine in men.

While my bloke had started off as Mr Nice Guy, once I was hooked he started withdrawing and I began running after him for more. More of what? The hugs were long gone, and the compliments had been replaced by insults almost on a daily basis. He turned out to be bad for me. I wasted more years of my life as a relationship addict than I care to admit.

The most important thing the books Brenda recommended gave me was the realisation that I need to get a grip. I needed to move away from that which is bad for me, and to stop craving it like a woman demented. I needed to find and build a healthy way of thinking. I needed balance, boundaries. I needed to stop my life from revolving around some misogynistic piece of *dreck*.

And so by getting honest and searching within, I began to understand Angela better. I began to learn about boundaries. I began to catch myself when I was making excuses for her, trying to control or avoid the truth. As a result, I began to stop enabling her. I was finally beginning to understand. Slowly I began to get healthy.

CHAPTER 22

Hard truths

In the writing of this book I have discovered many hard truths about my daughter. She has told me how for most of her teenage life she was resentful and angry, filled with rage and pain. She has told me that she always knew she preferred girls to boys, but dated Boyfriend because it was something she felt she needed to do for Ma and me. She blamed me a lot for our 'not-so-great' relationship and she spoke of how, as a result of her anger and shame, she built impenetrable walls around her.

I had also never known, until Angela mentioned it, that she had stopped fasting on *Yom Kippur*. I knew she had grown away from all her *Yiddishkeit* over the years, but even the most irreligious Jews fast on the holiest of all holy days, our Day of Atonement. The day when we bow down to *Hashem* to forgive us for our sins. It's such a solemn day, we are signed and sealed in *Hashem's* Book of Life.

'Who will live, and who will die?' we chant in the solemn prayer '*Unetane Tokeff*'. It was such a shock to me when she confessed this, but I had promised her when I started writing this book initially in collaboration with her – and then continued with it on my own – that I would never pass a negative comment, just listen and stay open minded. I know she found it very difficult, sharing those innermost secrets and thoughts. I know, but I kept my face focused on my computer screen and showed no reaction other than being happy that she was sharing her story with me.

'So, when did you actually start then? The drugs, I mean.'

She told me that she smoked dope and drank a bit in her teens but nothing 'hectic'. But when she was 20 she started smoking dope on weekends with her friends, then weekends turned to every night and every night became every day.

'Smoking took me away from myself, and I loved that,' she said. Once she started to tell me, she couldn't stop.

I hung out with my new gay hairdresser friend every weekend and I had my first ecstasy tablet and I loved it. Life was good. The ecstasy was accompanied by several joints and plenty tequila. For a small-framed girl I learned quickly how to keep up with him and pretty soon the average weekend started on Thursday night and continued non-stop until Sunday night when I would eventually pass out from exhaustion. By 2003, my hairdresser friend and I moved in together, much to my mother's dismay: what would the community think about me living with my gay best friend? I didn't give a fuck. In fact, that kind of talk added more fuel to my rebellious fire.

By now I was smoking dope every day, experimenting with acid and ecstasy, magic mushrooms and tried cocaine for the first time. But I didn't like it that much. Coke left me feeling anxious and uncontrollable, almost as if I was having a panic attack.

I had been working as a dental hygienist at the same practice for the past nine years and, apart from the daily dope, I started breathing in nitrous oxide. Because I worked alone and hardly got to speak to my patients or interact with many people, I managed to successfully hide the fact that I was using.

I felt bored with life and believed that I had reached the top professionally. I couldn't grow any more unless I went on to study dentistry, which I didn't want to do, or changed professional paths completely.

Then, on 24 October 2013, while I was having coffee with Angela and Ma in Europa, South Road, in Morningside – just four days before we were due to send this book off to a prospective publisher – Angela handed me a plastic bag full of handwritten pages.

'The Story of Me', she told me. 'I want you to read it. Maybe you can add some to the book – it might help you understand some things. I am warning you, though, there's a lot of it that you won't like.'

I was shaken, but I also felt honoured that she was finally trusting me with everything. She trusted me.

I drove home, and almost immediately I started reading. She was right, I didn't like a lot of it, but it was her story, and that's how she felt, that is how it was for her, how she saw and perceived her actions and deeds.

One thing was clear: I had not for one moment, in my wildest of wild, wild dreams, ever thought that so much of what had gone on in our lives, had affected her the way it had.

Maybe deep down I did know, but blocked it out. One thing that I read in the pages she gave me, that I had quite forgotten, was how even before Boyfriend, while she was still at school, she had been attracted to women. I think I really blocked that out. In earlier chapters when I wrote about the whole coming out around the time we thought she was getting engaged and how shocked I was when she first 'came out of the closet', I realised now while reading her writing how delusional I was when writing that. I could so easily just go back to that part and change it, correct it, but I have chosen not to, because that is how I believed it when I wrote it. It forced me to remember how, as a teenager, Angela had at times veered towards women.

I well remember a relationship she had with a girl, Dee Tee. At the time she had said it was just 'one of those things' and after a consultation with a top Johannesburg psychiatrist (which she resented) – who assured me that she was not gay but just 'experimenting' – I didn't think too much about it after that, particularly as she was dating Boyfriend then.

I read and read more about my daughter's secret thoughts and feelings and it became achingly clear to me what had hurt her in her growing-up years. Why did I never see it? If only I could have that time over again, I would have done so many things differently. Her writing brought up so much emotion in me. It broke my heart when I read how she had felt when she lost her sister.

On Wednesday, 7 April 2004, my life was to change forever. My sister Sam was a beautiful soul, people gravitated towards her, and she had a smile that could light up a room. I always told her that she was an old soul in a young body and often confided in her and sought her advice. She was wise beyond her years.

On 5 April, Sam was rushed to hospital. She had been complaining of flu-like symptoms, but when the headaches were so painful and so intense that she couldn't lift her head from the pillow, my dad drove her to the hospital. In the 20-minute drive from the house to Rosebank Clinic she became delirious and had a seizure. By the time they arrived at the hospital she had slipped into a coma and wasn't breathing. She was put onto life support. She couldn't breathe on her own. The doctors diagnosed her with bacterial meningitis. She had a 0–01% chance of survival and if she did come out of the coma she would be brain dead.

The doctors said we should prepare for the worst and if there was no change in 48 hours, they suggested we turn off the life support. Whilst my family camped out at the hospital, I needed to escape. I needed something, anything to numb the pain. I made a call, told my family I was going home to shower and change and off I went to buy CAT. Whilst my sister was fighting for her life, I was busy using CAT to take away the pain. I carry the shame and guilt to this day.

I went back to the hospital high on CAT, stoned on dope and completely detached from my emotions and the stark reality that awaited me.

This went on for two days and on 7 April 2004, at 10.30am, my family were all gathered around her bed so that we could say our goodbyes before the life support machine was turned off. Sam died, my beautiful sister, and something inside me died too – it was just four days before my 29th birthday, and almost seven weeks before Sam's 20th birthday.

I was angry, angry at a 'Benevolent G-d' who took the life of a beautiful soul, angry at the doctors who couldn't save her, angry at my dad and Felicité when the life support machines were turned off, but most of all angry at myself for betraying my sister, disrespecting her through my self-centred and selfish ways. She was busy dying and I was getting high.

The days after her passing were a drug blur. I smoked dope like cigarettes, snorted gram after gram after gram of CAT. I drank litres of anything I could lay my hands on.

I would spend the next seven days of Shiva (the Jewish mourning period) with my family and I was completely out of it.

The day of her funeral, I smoked the biggest joint I could make, had a few lines, and made sure my friend Lynda had her hip flask filled to the brim so that I could have a couple gulps of whisky. To this day I struggle to let go of the shame and humiliation and guilt I carry for not showing my beloved sister the respect she deserved. If you are listening, sweet Sam, I'm so sorry, sorry, sorry.

I used her death as an excuse to go out and use.

By now I was on a daily diet of CAT and dope. I hardly ate, lost plenty of weight, and wasn't sleeping much at all. I was now using so much that I was spending way beyond my means to support my habit. I stopped paying bills so that there was extra money for drugs. I got myself deeper and deeper into debt and had debt collectors calling on a daily basis.

I avoided everyone and isolated myself – and this continued for months and months. I eventually stopped isolating, but not the drugs. I tried to stop using so much and managed to cut down to a few joints a day and a gram of CAT, but the debt was out of control and I started stealing money from my family and, before long, the CAT was back up to two grams a day pushing three. R100 here or there was no longer sufficient and I started stealing money and jewellery from my family. I would steal anything that I could pawn, from gold earrings to family heirlooms.

I felt a slight pang of guilt at the time but the desire to use was far greater and won every time.

On Friday, 6 April, the day before the eighth year anniversary of her passing, I wrote my sister a letter, went to her grave site to read it to her, and asked her to help me to forgive myself for this, to help me get closure.

I went on to read more. The parts where she wrote in detail about how she stole and took what wasn't hers from everyone or anyone who happened to cross her path were particularly hard for me to stomach.

The first time I pawned something I crossed the I'll-never-do-that line. I kept telling myself that I'd buy it back as soon I had the money. It never occurred to me that I would never have the money.

It's funny how addiction can do that to you. I started with my own jewellery, a ring, a pair of gold earrings I got for my Bat Mitzvah from my Uncle Robert and Auntie Sharon, then a bracelet, and another bracelet. And then when I ran out of my own jewellery, I moved on to Mommy's things. Not that she had much, but whatever she did have, I took. She asked me once if I had felt guilty, and the answer was NO, I didn't, not in the least, because in my screwed-up head I was going to get the money and bail it all out again, so I was merely borrowing it. To be honest, maybe I felt a slight pang of guilt at the time but the desire to use was far greater and won every time.

… It was easy enough for me to do, take things. Friday night once at Mommy, after our Shabbos meal, I went upstairs and took it out of her little jewellery box. She'd never miss it, I told myself, as she hardly wore any jewellery at all. She only had a few pieces, they were all meaningful to her, and I took them.

Had I stopped for one moment to work it out logically, it would have been apparent that I could never ever get any of the jewellery out of the pawn shops. Not mine, not Mommy's.

I also took my brother's ring – a ring Mommy had given him for his Bar Mitzvah, which he left in his room once during one of his trips home to South Africa. A vague thought went through my head that Mommy would have a fit when she found out, but I didn't care. I needed the money for my all-consuming habit.

It wasn't long before I was stealing dollars and pounds from my boss. Because she travelled to the USA and UK regularly, we always had dollars and pounds in the office. Surely they wouldn't notice? Almost R60 000 later, they sure did. I denied it when confronted but after I failed the polygraph test, and before I was fired, I resigned... running away again. Not taking responsibility and facing up to my actions. I lied to my family and told them that I resigned because the working conditions were ridiculous. It was like slave labour and I deserved better. They bought it. [Fiancée] was a little less understanding as she knew we had a wedding and honeymoon to pay for but I talked myself out of that and she eventually saw my point of view. I was now unemployed with an R11 200-a-month drug habit and the lies and the stealing intensified.

What I did next I'm so ashamed of as this was the one person I swore I'd never steal from, never lie to, my gran. She always put me up on a pedestal and I do love her and always feared falling from grace in her eyes, especially if she knew the truth about me. I feared failing in her eyes, yet I did. I lied to her, manipulated her, stole from her and betrayed her trust in me.

I also took things from her and pawned them. It was so easy. She would be making supper for us and I'd go into her room, go through her drawers and take whatever I thought I could get money for. Traveller's cheques, foreign currency not that it was much, but it was hers. But I didn't see it that way at all. Often when my gran was not home, I went in there and helped myself to her jewellery.

Whatever I found went right up my nose.

When I went into treatment I realised how much shame and guilt I had been suppressing around all the things I had done. I was especially petrified and fearful over my gran's reaction when she found out I was a drug addict, and about all the things I had stolen from her. About how I had lied to her and how I was now in rehab. I didn't care that everyone else knew I stole, and that I was a raging addict, but I did care if my gran did.

What were we going to tell her about my not being able to be at our Wednesday-night suppers? I knew that she was going to have to learn the truth, and that Mommy was going to have to tell her. I just couldn't. Keeping the truth from her all these years put me in a very bad head space, imagining her judgement of me, which I assumed she would cast my way, but which she actually never did.

Initially my family had decided to keep it from her because they were worried about her health and felt that this would be harmful to her. I was relieved and grateful.

By now I had lied to, betrayed and stolen from pretty much everyone in my life. It was only when backed into a corner that I would eventually get honest. I had broken trust with everyone, and no one believed a word that came out of my mouth.

When I was arrested and held in the cells for the weekend, sitting in a cold cell I had a moment of clarity. They say that, while using, an addict is headed for 'jails, institutions and death'. I had already been to rehab once. I was now sitting in jail – my moment of clarity hit me right between the eyes. If I carried on this road my next stop was death. Do not pass Begin, do not collect R200.

My mother eventually had to tell my gran the truth – and she was shattered. She didn't want to talk to me and she questioned the integrity and sincerity of my love for her. My biggest fear had become my reality. I had betrayed the one person I cherished the most. The pain I experienced was nothing like anything I had ever felt before. I feel so ashamed and humiliated for having lied to her, stolen from her and deceived her. Of all my consequences, losing my gran's trust and respect is the one that cuts the deepest and hurts the most.

The day when Mommy told me that my gran didn't want to talk to me 'for the moment', I went through intense cravings in rehab because I couldn't handle the feelings of possible rejection and abandonment, things I didn't want to feel. For a moment I thought it would have been easier to just 'use'.

[But] I was relieved to at least be in rehab during this time. I felt safe there, and most important of all, the lies could now stop, the lies would come out in the open, I could get that clean slate that I needed and I could start again, one day at a time. They say

that secrets keep you sick. It was only when I started to get honest that I started getting well.

On the day I left rehab, I went to see my gran. I needed to start taking accountability for my actions. Confronting my biggest fear allowed me the opportunity to start a new life with a clean and honest slate. It proved to be a good place to start rebuilding all the damage and chaos I'd caused. Slowly but surely I began getting honest with myself and those around me, which allowed me to make real connections with my friends and family.

Working on this book with my mom helped me get perspective and clarity. I began to see the progression of my disease, the insanity and, most of all, the darkness that constantly engulfed me. Where I was once completely depleted through my using, today I know more than anything else: I want a life.

My name is Angela Shannon Brest and I am a grateful recovering addict.

Afterword

Angela has come a long, long way. As I write this she has been clean for over two years. Just for today.

She is happily living with her girlfriend Stephanie and their little kittens, Oliver and Miss Lola, and their little grey rabbit, Kayla. They have a lovely townhouse in North Riding, a quiet suburb of Randburg. They have a little bedroom all done out for J, Stephanie's five-year-old daughter, so that when the child comes to stay she has her own room. Their home has a warm feel to it, with a great vibe, no more chaos or mess, no cigarettes lying around in ashtrays for days on end, no more dirt, no more crumpled-up bits of paper. It's a normal household.

My daughter is part of a family unit filled with love and light. She has direction, she knows that her life over the last 10 years or so was utter chaos, but now she also knows where she is going. She has picked herself up and moved on, towards a bright future and, G-d willing, a good life.

I cannot even begin to imagine how difficult it must have been for her. Over the past two years I have watched Angela put her heart and soul into her sobriety; she has worked so hard to get clean and to stay clean. All I know about addiction is from what I have read, as well as the experiences I have had in obsessive relationships, but they are nothing compared to what Angela has experienced. I don't know how it must be for her emotionally. I can only try to imagine. Writing this book and talking a lot to her during this time has taught me so much about my daughter. And myself. We have shared so much together – stuff that, up until I began writing this, neither of us had ever spoken about properly.

I have learned so much since first finding out that Angela was using drugs. I learned that Angela's needs must be her own number-one priority. She must come first. She will need to go to her meetings for many, many more years to come, maybe even forever, because it is so easy to slip back into her old ways. Even though meetings and re-enforcements and her various mantras will get her through, it is still going to be a difficult road. And even though she is clean today, who knows what tomorrow may bring, or the day after that, or the year after that. There is never a 'home and dry'. My grandfather gave up cigarettes for 30 years and then went back to smoking just like that. So addiction is just that – there is no logic, and mostly there is little or no thought of the consequences.

I have also learned that addiction is the continued repetition of destructive behaviour, despite obviously negative consequences, and that drugs have untold powers over their victims. Like a hypnotist has over a volunteer at a show, the drug wields its power over the addict. They say that under hypnosis a person would never go so far as to do something that they wouldn't do in normal everyday life, something that went against their morals and principals, but drugs are much more powerful than that because they rob the addict of all perspective, principals and morals.

Today I understand that drug addiction is a preventable disease. Research has shown that prevention programmes involving families, schools, communities, and the media are very effective in reducing drug abuse.

Instead of subjects in school that have little or no use to the learner in later life, I have often asked why Drug Prevention isn't taught as a subject. Daily. Drug awareness in schools shouldn't be just about having a recovering addict come in and give a talk to the learners once a year. Drug Education/Prevention should be taught at schools every single day. Movies should be made of 'ordinary people' with 'ordinary lives' who have been ensnared by the world of drugs, to show what this does to them, to their families – nothing should be held back when showing the destroyed lives, wasted moments, wasted hours, wasted years caused by drugs. The long, hard struggle to clean up and 'come back' into society again as a whole functioning person should be what we teach our children – and no details should be spared.

These movies/documentaries should show people who have caused untold damage to their brain, show how they never come right, how some even end up in special care facilities, needing special attention and medical assistance.

I would like to see movies like this on the cinema circuit, not starring famous actors like the Brad Pitts or Johnny Depps, but ordinary, unglamorous people who have been through the drug mill, through the nightmare of addiction, people who may even still be using, and people who have cleaned up their act and no longer dancing with drugs.

There are no short cuts, Angela often says. She also says giving up the drugs doesn't make her 'clean'. It's all the gunge inside her head, stuff lying there for years and years, never having been dealt with, that needs attention. Recovery is all about dealing with all of these things. I can only imagine how hard it's been for her, to sit and thrash out her life, over and over to her counsellor, revealing to me such intimate and hard-to-share details, relentlessly delving into the deepest corners of her self. But it's vital that she does this, for hers was a huge festering wound that needed to be cleaned out, properly. All has to go, nothing can be left behind.

Sometimes I catch myself getting embroiled in self-pity, anger and blame for having to deal with all the fallout from Angela's addiction. But I know I need to get over myself. Although I know that nothing she did was against any of us personally, I am still upset about Gregory's *Bar Mitzvah* ring, and Lionel's Kruger rands. I know those are material things, and I know I should move on, but still it's difficult for me. I work hard on trying to rid my own mind of the occasional bouts anger and resentment, the why-did-you-have-to-do-it that surfaces every now and then.

One day when working on this book together we took a short break.

'Ang, what are we going to do about Granny? We still haven't told her about the uh... prison part of it – we have to tell her.'

'Mommy, we will. I will, I'll do it, nearer the time,' she answered as she sipped a glass of cold water with fresh mint Helen had picked from the vegetable garden.

I felt the tears well up in my eyes. She really was changing, owning this, taking responsibility for telling Ma. I was always the one who had to get Ma through the challenges we all faced, but now Angela was starting to take that upon herself. I could see before my very eyes that she was becoming a whole person again, her mind clear. Gone was the aggression, the snappiness, the abrasive way she spoke to me over the last few years. This filled my heart with such joy. I am convinced treatment is vital to recovery; rehab – if it can be afforded – teaches the addict how to deal with addiction one day at a time, until the addict emerges as a whole person once again. But it's a long and very difficult struggle. There is no easy way. Addicts have to muster up every ounce of strength within them to fight their addiction, those parasitic demons, to shake them off, clear out their minds, their bodies, and their souls.

I believe that rehab, in tandem with NA meetings, is the way forward. They say recovery works on those who want to work it.

As I look at Angela, I see the fruits of her recovery growing before my eyes. And I am so grateful to her for turning her life around, for regaining faith in herself, for having climbed out of that very dark and very black hole she had dug for herself. I am grateful to her for attending her meetings, for listening to her counsellors, her sponsor, for walking the talk, for cleaning up her act, for getting me to learn to trust her again, and most of all, for all her hard work and dedication to getting clean.

I am grateful to her, too, for allowing me to witness her soul, her darkest secrets in the writing of this book. Sharing 'The Story of Me' with me has been a hugely positive and cathartic experience in my life – and, I suspect, in hers too. I sometimes wish I had seen it earlier, but I have stopped berating myself for my denial and have accepted that it all had to do with G-d's timing. It took Rabbi Abraham Twerski, a professor of psychiatry, 50 years to finally understand the addictive personality. 'Addiction,' he sad, 'is not shameful. Denial is.'

After much questioning and struggling with the concept, I have finally come to accept and understand that addiction is a disease that affects the entire family; it reaches out its tentacles and touches each and every one. Like a curse, a cancer, it has played havoc with all our lives.

I spent days, weeks, months, years in introspection, digging deep into my memory, trying to relive the last 38 years from the time Angela was born, and among many things, I have learned from Angela that her low self-esteem stems largely from the knowledge that she is gay and felt she had to hide it from the world in order to avoid rejection from her family and her community. The other significant source of pain is that she missed out on Hymie being part of her everyday life.

A few days before I finished writing this book, I decided to call Hymie.

'Hello, Woosh, I need to speak to you,' I said.

'I'm just on my way into a meeting, Annie, What's it about?'

'Woosh, just come over, I need to speak to you.' I explained that I wanted to speak to him face to face, and not over the phone, not on Facebook and not on WhatsApp.

It took two weeks of various no-shows but he finally came over.

'What's so important that it couldn't be said over the phone?' he said sniffing the banana bread Helen was just taking out of the oven.

'It's about Angela...'

'Is she using again?' he asked, and at the same time asked Helen to cut him a slice of her banana bread.

'No, she's not, but we do need to talk. You see…' I paused. 'I've written this book, as you know, and now I'm at the end of it, and I would like you to do something – something for Angela…'

I told him that while I really did appreciate that he paid for the rehab, I wanted something from him more important than money. I told him I wanted him to add something to the book, something for Angela by way of a message, something she had waited to hear her whole life but had never heard. He told me to type up something myself and he'd have a look at it. But that is not what this was about. I didn't want to write it for him, I wanted it to be his thoughts, not mine, his voice. I wanted it to come directly from him, from his heart, this message for his daughter.

I suggested that he just talk, and I would type. I had said everything I wanted to say in the book and, as a result, I felt I had found closure, but had he?

'Okay, I need to think about this, what I want to say,' he said, pouring himself another cup of coffee.

'Woosh, do it – and do it now. Angela has waited many years for this…'

'I'm not a writer, I'm no good at expressing my feelings, you know *me*.' I suddenly realised he was nervous; he was not used to expressing himself, giving a voice to his feelings.

'Do it, Woosh, I'm waiting.'

I walked over to my laptop, sat down, and waited for him.

Hymie is not an emotional man, one who wears his heart on his sleeve. I have seen him cry only twice in my life, once at the birth of our son, and the second at the funeral of his beloved daughter, Samantha. As he sat down, he was so emotional that I was almost sorry I had pushed him to this point. But he pulled himself together and spoke out.

Angi, this is Dad. You're the sweetest little thing and I love you very, very much.

I'm grateful that you had your mother and grandmother there for you when you were growing up. I know it should have been me, Angi, but things are hard to explain and I don't have any excuses. If I could live my life over again, I promise you I would do things very differently.

But please know one thing – you are no different to any of the other kids I have. I am truly sorry for the pain I have caused you, and I know that I have. But again, I love you, I truly do. I know that it may not always look like it.

I want you to know that I'm always here for you and if ever you need to talk to me or want to buy me a coffee, I'm always available.

And even though I wasn't there for you throughout your growing-up years you were always – and will always – be a very special and brave girl in my life.

I'm very proud of the way you've come through all your problems and I am proud to tell people what you have achieved.

I love you lots and lots.

Your Dad. x

Recovery is all about growing and moving forward, about taking responsibility for the hurt we may have caused, and trying to change the patterns. As much as it's a family disease, it is also a wonderful opportunity for families to heal.

The greatest gift you could ever have given us, Angela, is that just for today you are 'clean and serene'. There is nothing in this world I want more than your health and happiness and for you to stay on this road of recovery that you continue to follow through sheer determination.

Ang, I'm proud of you. I'm sorry for all the things I may have done wrong, even for some of the heated discussions we had while working on this book together. But we came through it with flying colours, didn't we?

Rock on, Angela!

Love always,

Mommy xxxx

Author's note

Nothing I have written on these pages was meant to be judgemental – neither was it meant to be a pity party. I have written about what happened, and it hasn't been easy. I am still not over a lot of it, and at times I still feel hurt and anger.

Writing about it has helped me, helped Angela, and hopefully it will help you, or someone you know who was or is in the same boat. Everything I have shared here is in the hope that someone may see him- or herself here too. A lot of what I have written is how I see it, and I'm sure others may well see it differently – we can't all see everything the same way, but this is how I see it, how I experienced it, what I have learned from it. My wish, please G-d, is for someone else who finds themselves in the position I was in to be able to benefit from this story.

I salute all those who have managed to escape the clutches of drugs and alcohol, and I implore those who have never used not to start. Don't try it. Don't do it. It's not cool, not smart, not sophisticated.

Here's to you, Angela, you have endured a long, hard and very painful struggle, but you have finally – with the help of the Twelve-Step programme, Houghton House and The Gap, your counsellor Alex Hamlyn and the people in the Fellowship, and through your own determination and courage – managed to stay clean. I salute you for that.

Acknowledgements

Thank you, Angela, for your courage and determination, and for allowing me to tell our story. I know it evoked a lot of pain and bad memories for you. I realise that I only started to truly understand what 'addiction' was all about when we started working on this book. I am honoured that you trusted me to write this. And I love you, Ang.

Ma – Julie Marcus Lapedus – thank you for the role you always played in the lives of my children. You were always their rock. You were more than a gran to them – you were their second mother. Sorry if I was impossible at times.

To my son, Gregory Brest, and special Mandy Pacheco, thank you both for reading the very first draft of this book, and for giving me the confidence to continue.

To my brother Robert and sister-in-law Sharon, thank you for all your help. I know it was hard for all of us, a very trying time, but for everything you did I am beyond grateful. And always will be.

My special love to my darling Auntie Freda, my beloved Brenda Y, and my darling Daphne J. I will always love you.

To my special friends, Joel K, Gilda G, Molly R, Carol Z, Patti from Pletti, Jenni T, Beile G, June E, Leora (G)B and my darling Helen Ledwaba. Thank you to all of you for your unconditional support and for not judging Angela during her dark days.

Hymie Brest. Thank you, Woosh, for helping me to end the book, and for your honesty in doing so, and of course for funding Angela's rehab. Thank you to Felicité and Tiffany Brest for your continued support and understanding when it came to the crunch.

To dear Rabbi and Rebbetzen Suchard of BHH Sandton, for your understanding and your kindness.

Rabbi David Shaw. Thank you, cousin Rabbi, for texting Angela each and every Friday afternoon without fail. It meant a lot to her, and to me – a small gesture with a meaning of giant proportions.

To Alex Hamlyn of Houghton House/The Gap, I cannot thank you enough for everything you did for Angela, for being her counsellor and for helping her work towards a healthy and better place. You're terrific!

Gaye Turiel, you were the first person I came to see with Angela, for guidance. Thank you also for your Codependency/Enabling Group. I still read your notes.

Barbara, being part of your tough love group was a very special time in my life. Thank you for caring, for being so amazing, and thank you for everything I learned from you. I really love you, Barbie.

To Lionel G, beloved partner, we travelled a difficult road, I know. I love you.

Stephanie, thank you for making my girl so happy! That means everything to me.

Sponsor, you were really great, and I know you really cared for Angela. Thank you for all the times we spoke and for your fierce loyalty to my daughter. I will always treasure that memory.

New Sponsor. Thank you. I know Angela holds you in very high esteem! Hugs.

Sean Fraser, you are a genius. The Best. I cannot thank you enough for editing this book. I have learned so much from you. You are amazing.

And last, but certainly not least, a huge thank-you to you, Melinda Ferguson of MFBooks/Jacana Media, for your encouragement, your unstinting frankness and honesty, your dogged persistence in pushing me to tell the whole story, and not just the parts I had chosen to tell. Thank you for the many hours you spent editing – there were days I was terrified to come to the computer and see your red and purple pen marks pointing to everything I still needed to attend to. I hope I didn't drive you too mad with my loony habit of using capital letters... I think you're the only person to call me a lunatic and get away with it!

Anne Lapedus Brest